THE CRY OF A STONE

by Anna Trapnel

Medieval and Renaissance Texts and Studies

Volume 220

HANNAH TRAPNEL,
a Quaker, and pretended Prophetess.
(From a scarce Print by Gaywood)

ANNA TRAPNEL

The caption is misleading: Trapnel was reputed as a Fifth-Monarchist prophet.

Richard Gaywood (fl. 1650–1680) was a well-known engraver, whose work also included portraits of Charles I, Oliver Cromwell, and Charles II.
The print is reproduced by permission of the
Syndics of Cambridge University Library, from Rare Book Syn.7.65.157.

THE CRY OF A STONE

by Anna Trapnel

edited and introduced by

Hilary Hinds

Arizona Center for Medieval and Renaissance Studies
Tempe, Arizona
2000

Library of Congress Cataloging-in-Publication Data

Trapnel, Anna.
   The cry of a stone / by Anna Trapnel ; edited and introduced by Hilary
   Hinds.
       p. cm. — (Medieval & Renaissance texts & studies ; v. 220)
   Includes bibliographical references and index.
   ISBN 0-86698-262-0 (alk. paper)
       1. Great Britain—Politics and government—1649-1660—Sources.
   2. Fifth Monarchy Men—Sources. I. Hinds, Hilary. II. Title. III. Medieval
   & Renaissance Texts & Studies (Series) ; v. 220.
   DA420.T73 2000
   941.06'3.—dc21
                                                                    00-045357

∞
This book is made to last.
It is set in Goudy, smyth-sewn,
and printed on acid-free paper
to library specifications.

Printed in the United States of America

For Anna

CONTENTS

ACKNOWLEDGEMENTS

I am grateful to Cheltenham and Gloucester College of Higher Education for granting me a semester's study leave in 1998, during which time I was able to complete the work on this edition.

I would like to acknowledge the help of the staff of the following libraries in the UK and USA: Birmingham University Library; Bodleian Library, Oxford; British Library; Cambridge University Library; University of Chicago Library, Illinois; William Andrews Clark Memorial Library, UCLA; Earlham College Library, Richmond, Indiana; Edinburgh University Library; the Library of the Society of Friends, London; Folger Shakespeare Library, Washington D.C.; Houghton Library, Harvard University, Cambridge, Massachusetts; Haverford College Library, Haverford, Pennsylvania; Henry E. Huntington Library, San Marino, California; Founders' Library, University of Wales, Lampeter; Magdalen College Library, Cambridge; University of Minnesota Library, Minneapolis, Minnesota; Swarthmore College Library, Swarthmore, Pennsylvania; Worcester College Library, Oxford. Thanks also to James R. Sewell, City Archivist at the Corporation of London Records Office.

I would also like to thank Elspeth Graham for suggesting that I undertake the work on this edition, Sue Wiseman and Penny Richards for help with references, Maureen Bell for her bibliographic help, Gordon McConville and Thorsten Moritz for their help with elucidating biblical references and the specificities of Calvinism, and June Roberts for her original transcription of the text. Thanks are also due to my two anonymous readers at Medieval and Renaissance Texts and Studies, whose comments were encouraging, incisive and helpful, and to Leslie S. B. MacCoull, my expert copy-editor. The greatest debt of gratitude is, as always, to Jackie Stacey, for her unfaltering encouragement, even in the face of what must at times seem a strange preoccupation with a distant century.

INTRODUCTION

Anna Trapnel's *The Cry of a Stone* is a prophecy, written in the middle of the turbulent years of the English Revolution, in 1654. To someone approaching this text now, the prospect of reading a prognostication the accuracy of which we, some three hundred and fifty years later, might test, or marvel at, may promise an intriguing, even tantalising, encounter.

Such expectations will almost certainly be confounded by this particular prophecy. One reason for this is that "prophecy" in the seventeenth century meant something quite different from what it does now. "Prophecy" for us suggests the prognostication of events; whilst there certainly were such "prophecies" in the seventeenth century, concerned to foretell the future in the secular and often political sense that we now associate with this activity,[1] prophecy at that time usually had an overtly religious dimension, and as such had a range of more diverse meanings. At its broadest, "prophecy was any utterance produced by God through human agency."[2] This might mean, as Mary Cary (like Trapnel, a Fifth-Monarchist prophet writing in the 1650s) suggested, that "all might prophesy, that is (in the lowest sense) be able to speak to edification, exhortation and comfort."[3] By this definition, "prophecy" elides with preaching (though neither activity was confined to ministers), but the naming of something as "prophecy" conferred on it a kind of authority and mystique

---

[1] Tim Thornton, "Reshaping the Local Future: The Development and Uses of Provincial Political Prophecies, 1300–1900," in *Prophecy: The Power of Inspired Language in History 1300–2000*, ed. Bertrand Taithe and Tim Thornton (Stroud, Glos.: Sutton Publishing, 1997), 51–67.

[2] Diane Purkiss, "Producing the Voice, Consuming the Body: Women Prophets of the Seventeenth Century," in *Women, Writing, History 1640–1740*, ed. Isobel Grundy and Susan Wiseman (London: Batsford, 1992), 139–58, here 139.

[3] Mary Cary, *A New and More Exact Mappe or Description of New Jerusalems Glory* (London, 1651), 237.

beyond that available to utterances associated only with human agency.
However, "prophecy" also had more precise, and more contentious, meanings: it signified words inspired by or emanating from God, where the
human medium was no more than a mouthpiece for his words. The prophet is thus, as Trapnel says, "made a voice, a sound, it is a voice within a
voice, another's voice, even thy voice through her" (p. 45).[4] Trapnel's
prophecies are striking (though not unique) for being uttered, more often
than not, in trances and, at times, in verse;[5] however, they are in the
mainstream of prophetic utterances at this time for being a place for the
expression of sentiments of dissent or opposition, whether to the monarchy, Parliament, the army, Cromwell, the clergy, the inhabitants of a
 particular city or town, or the "ungodly" more generally. Thus, it has
been argued, prophecy provided a means by which, in the middle years of
the seventeenth century, women were able to intervene in public relig-
ious/political debates and events to an unprecedented extent: Phyllis Mack
suggests that "over four hundred women prophesied at least once during
the second half of the seventeenth century, about 375 of whom were
Quakers."[6] As God's chosen instruments, they were able to claim for
themselves positions beyond the conventionally feminine.[7]

Whilst by this account prophecy might not be straightforwardly
predictive (though there may be an element of this), it would almost certainly demonstrate an interest in the future in one way or another; as
Watt suggests,

---

[4] All page numbers to *The Cry of a Stone* given in this introduction refer to this edition.

[5] Sarah Wight also prophesied in a trance: see Barbara Ritter Dailey, "The Visitation of
Sarah Wight: Holy Carnival and the Revolution of the Saints in Civil War London," *Studies
in Church History* 55 (1986): 438–55.

[6] Phyllis Mack, "The Prophet and Her Audience: Gender and Knowledge in The World
Turned Upside Down," in *Reviving the English Revolution: Reflections and Elaborations on the
Work of Christopher Hill*, ed. Geoff Eley and William Hunt (London: Verso, 1988), 139–52,
here 150, n. 1.

[7] For recent discussions of this aspect of women's prophecies from the seventeenth century, see Phyllis Mack, "Women as Prophets During the English Civil War," in *The Origins
of Anglo-American Radicalism*, ed. Margaret Jacob and James Jacob (London: George Allen and
Unwin, 1984), 214–30; Phyllis Mack, "The Prophet and Her Audience"; Phyllis Mack, *Vi-
sionary Women: Ecstatic Prophecy in Seventeenth-Century England* (Berkeley, CA: University of
California Press, 1992); Elaine Hobby, *Virtue of Necessity: English Women's Writing 1649–1688*
(London: Virago, 1988); Elaine Hobby, "The Politics of Women's Prophecy in the English
Revolution," in *Sacred and Profane: Secular and Devotional Interplay in Early Modern British
Literature*, ed. Helen Wilcox et al. (Amsterdam: Free University Press, 1996), 295–306; Nigel
Smith, *Perfection Proclaimed: Language and Literature in English Radical Religion 1640–1660* (Ox-
ford: Clarendon Press, 1989); Purkiss, "Producing the Voice, Consuming the Body"; Hilary
Hinds, *God's Englishwomen: Seventeenth-Century Radical Sectarian Writing and Feminist Criticism*
(Manchester: Manchester University Press, 1996); Diane Watt, *Secretaries of God: Women
Prophets in Late Medieval and Early Modern England* (Cambridge: D. S. Brewer, 1997).

It might commit God to a certain course of events by predicting
the future, proclaiming God's word or interpreting Scripture, and it
might also require those to whom it was addressed and sometimes
the prophet her/himself to take action.[8]

This interest in the future, however, is manifested in and through an intense preoccupation with the past; in particular, it is concerned with reading signs from the past in relation to the present in order to recommend
or assert a particular kind of future. For most prophets of the seventeenth
century, Trapnel included, the key sign to be read was the Bible: what she
graphically calls "the entrails of scripture" (p. 17) are to be examined for
the understanding they will offer up of contemporary events and the implications of these for the future. Similarly, historical events, political manoeuvres, natural phenomena, dreams, and visions are to be examined and
interpreted; read aright, all have the power to unlock the mysterious sig-
nificances of God's providential plan.

The future in which Trapnel is interested is, in the first instance, the
immediate one, though this is of interest only because of its implications
for the longer-term future and the establishment of the Fifth Monarchy
(see p. xxvii): she is concerned with the question of what is to become of
God's chosen nation now that Cromwell, who had seemed destined to lead
God's people into the promised land, has betrayed the cause by taking on
the mantle of Lord Protector. Her answer to this question is dependent on
the authority conferred by two areas of signification and the interpretations she offers of them: first, her readings of biblical texts (particularly
the prophecies of Daniel and Revelation); and second, her own visions
(*The Cry of a Stone* was uttered whilst Trapnel was in a trance, and details
several instances of her own divinely inspired prophetic dreams and visions) and her capacity to persuade her audience and readership of their
godly origin. The future that Trapnel sets forth in the prophecy, then, is
utterly dependent on a correct reading of the "past" of the Bible and the
"present" of the mode and circumstances of the prophetic pronounce-
ment. Such a definition of "prophecy" presents a challenge to the modern
reader in that it does not allow us the easy pleasures afforded by the privileged position of retrospective judgement, the award of credit and debit
points based on our assessment of the prophet's accuracy of prediction. Instead, we are called on to rethink our own definitions of the genre, to consider it as a means of staking a claim in a particular version of the past,
present and future, and to reassess the kinds of insights and pleasures that
it might offer.

---

[8] Watt, *Secretaries of God*, 2.

Another challenge offered to today's reader by *The Cry of a Stone* is the unfamiliarity of its style and structure. After a brief retrospective autobiographical introduction to Trapnel's life and prophetic credentials (pp. 6–15 below), we move into the substantial body of the prophecy itself, which can best be characterised as a series of non-linear, allusive, and reflexive meditations on the themes of betrayal and salvation. It comprises a mixture of topical reference (to Cromwell, repeatedly; to the army; to recent political events), biblical allusion, portentous warnings of impending doom for the ungodly of the nation, and ecstatic anticipation of the changes (spiritual, social and political) to be wrought by the second coming of Jesus; and it is written in loosely punctuated and syntactically unorthodox prose, and in verse whose scansion, diction, and phrasing display its extemporary origins. The difficulties occasioned for a modern reader by this style are likely to be compounded by the density of topical reference and the reliance on biblical allusion, for the text assumes a currency to both of these that, for most of us at least, is no longer the case. Such difficulties should, however, not be overemphasised; the writing also has a compelling momentum and urgency, and a sense of passion and outrage that speaks loud and clear across the historical divide.

The strangeness of this text, a result of its generic and stylistic unfamiliarity, as well as of its historical distance from us, constitutes both its difficulty and its appeal. It is the aim of this introduction to elucidate some of the difficulties, and to suggest some of the reasons why this text, after a long period of critical neglect, seems increasingly to preoccupy and fascinate scholars today. This unorthodox text is, I would suggest, best read with as full an understanding as possible of Anna Trapnel's life and situation, of the historical circumstances which gave rise both to the prophecy itself and to its specific meanings at this highly charged moment in the revolutionary decades of the mid-seventeenth century, and of the ways in which the text has figured (or failed to figure) in the historical and literary-historical record more recently. The introduction which follows falls accordingly into three parts. The first section offers a detailed discussion of Trapnel's own account of her life and work, and suggests some of the possibilities and problems offered by such material for our reading of the prophecy. The second section provides a brief historical contextualisation to the prophecy, and suggests some strategies for reading this unfamiliar mix of historical, religious, and political material. The final section traces the history of the twentieth-century critical reception of *The Cry of a Stone* by historians and literary critics, and suggests some reasons for the recent marked increase in critical interest in this and other prophetic writings from the seventeenth century.

"I AM ANNA TRAPNEL":
READING TRAPNEL'S LIFE AND WRITINGS

At the beginning of January 1654, Anna Trapnel moved suddenly and dramatically into the public eye. Attending the examination by the Council of State[9] at Whitehall of Vavasor Powell, a prominent Baptist/Fifth Monarchist preacher, she fell into a trance, and was taken to an inn nearby. The trance lasted eleven or twelve days,[10] during which time she sang, prayed and prophesied, attracting an increasingly large and high-profile crowd, including members of the Council of State, ex-Members of Parliament, ministers, and members of the aristocracy — a mix of sympathisers and sceptics — who came and listened to her each day. From the fifth day onwards, a member of her audience ("the relator" who features repeatedly in *The Cry of a Stone*) recorded her words.

Trapnel's fame spread, and continued to grow even once her trance was over. Marchamont Needham (or Nedham), for example, a journalist, pamphleteer and government supporter, wrote to Cromwell on 7 February:

> Wishing to know how the pulse beats at Allhallows,[11] I went there last night. It was a dull assembly without Feake or Simpson,[12] for they were the men that carried it on with heat. Highland, John Spencer, and Mr. Jessey,[13] who now conduct it, are no Boanerges,[14] as you know. But the congregation is crowded, the humours boiling, and as much scum comes off as ever, but more warily . . .
>
> There is a twofold design about the prophetess Hannah [Trapnel], who played her part lately at Whitehall at the ordinary;[15] one to print her discourses and hymns, which are desperate against your person, family, children, friends and the government; the

---

[9] The Council of State was the chief executive body instituted on 13 February 1649, following the execution of the king.

[10] The precise dates and duration of Trapnel's trance are hard to determine; see p. 82, note 6.

[11] Trapnel was a member of the Fifth-Monarchist congregation which met at John Simpson's church of Allhallows the Great in Thames Street.

[12] Christopher Feake and John Simpson were leading Fifth Monarchists, imprisoned in Windsor Castle since 28 January. See pp. 84, note 14, and 85, note 17.

[13] Samuel Highland was a Baptist lay preacher and a Parliamentary radical in the Barebones Parliament of 1653; he later sat in the Parliaments of 1654 and 1656. John Spencer was a Baptist and Fifth Monarchist, famous for his public preaching. Unlike many other Fifth Monarchists, he remained loyal to the Protectorate. Henry Jessey, also a Baptist and Fifth Monarchist, joined Feake and Simpson as a weekday lecturer at Allhallows in 1651; see p. 86, note 19.

[14] Boanerges means "sons of thunder"; James and John are so called by Christ in Mark 3.17.

[15] An ordinary was an eating house or tavern.

other to send her all over England, to proclaim them *vivâ voce*. She is much visited, and does a world of mischief in London, and would do in the country. The vulgar dote on vain prophecies. I saw hers in the hands of a man who was in the room when she uttered them day by day in her trance, as they call it. He promised to lend me them; if he does, I will show you them. They would make 14 or 15 sheets in print.[16]

Needham's note conveys a vivid sense of the febrile, gossip-driven, power-broking atmosphere of the capital at a time of constantly shifting political allegiances and coalitions; it trades a set of names which clearly carry their own highly charged meanings, and it demonstrates a contempt for those of the populace who support his political adversaries, as well as a sense of urgency, immediacy and volatility. It also indicates, however, that the activities of Trapnel and her congregation were perceived to be significant enough — and, more precisely, a sufficient threat to order and stable government — for Cromwell, installed only two months earlier as Lord Protector, to be given first-hand intelligence of them. This concern about the sedition and disorder that Trapnel's activities betokened culminated, in April of that year, in her arrest in Cornwall for "aspersing the government"; she was then transported by sea back to London, and imprisoned in Bridewell, from where she was released in July (see her work *Anna Trapnel's Report and Plea* [London, 1654]). Her reputation is suggested by the fact that her name appears in a number of contemporary newspapers, in the texts of other sectarian writers and prophets (both sympathetic and hostile), and by allusion in the political theorist and philosopher Thomas Hobbes's history of the Civil Wars, *Behemoth*.[17] Moreover, public appetite for accounts of her prophecies and activities were such that in 1654 four texts were published under her name: *Strange and Wonderful Newes from White-hall* (dated "March" by Thomason[18]) and *The Cry of a Stone* both give accounts of her prophetic trance in January of that year; *A Legacy for Saints* (dated "July 24" by Thomason) is a collection of accounts of Trapnel's conversion and early prophecies, written, we are told, "some years since with her own hand," and finishing with a number of letters

---

[16] *Calendar of State Papers: Domestic*; Marchamont Needham to the Protector, 7 February 1654.

[17] Although the first authorised edition of *Behemoth* was not published until 1682, it was written in 1668. For the allusion to Trapnel, see Thomas Hobbes, *Behemoth, or The Long Parliament*, ed. Ferdinand Tönnies (Chicago and London: University of Chicago Press, 1990), 187.

[18] George Thomason (d. 1666) was a London bookseller and publisher, who amassed a large collection of political tracts and broadsides published between the outbreak of the Civil War and the Restoration, some of which he annotated. His collection was donated to the British Museum in 1762.

sent by her from Cornwall; and *Anna Trapnel's Report and Plea* focuses on her travels to Cornwall and her subsequent imprisonment and return to London.

There had been few public foreshadowings of Trapnel's rapidly rising star before 1654. Whilst she had had visions and revelations prior to this — she recounts them in detail in *The Cry of a Stone*, interpreting them as relating to Cromwell, the army and its battles, the New Jerusalem and the second coming of King Jesus, her own sin and salvation — they had attracted little attention. She tells us that friends and acquaintances knew of them, but did not recognise them immediately for what they were. Some were troubled by them ("I was judged by some divers friends to be under a temptation" [p. 8]), whilst others reserved judgement: they "waited till they saw it accomplished, and then admired" (p. 9). Yet Trapnel's own account, at the beginning of *The Cry of a Stone*, of her spiritual pedigree, her credentials as a prophet, is unequivocal, presenting us with a progress narrative leading inexorably to this moment of public recognition and acceptance. First, she tells us that she was the daughter of godly parents, "living and dying in the profession of the Lord Jesus"; in particular, her mother's dying words — words which carried a particular and portentous weight within the Christian tradition[19] — marked Trapnel out as different, destined for a special relationship with God: "Lord! double thy spirit upon my child" (p. 6) (see Zechariah 9.9-12).[20] Second, during a serious illness in 1647, when she was "given over by all for dead," God promises her recovery by drawing her attention to the scriptures, to Hosea 6.2, which she paraphrases as "After two dayes I will revive thee, the third day I will raise thee up, and thou shalt live in my sight." Subsequently, she writes, "the Lord made use of me for the refreshing of afflicted and tempted ones, inwardly and outwardly" (p. 6), and, this accomplished, reveals to her the next stage of his plans: "in that thou hast been faithful in a little, I will make thee an instrument of much more; for particular souls shall not only have benefit of thee, but the universality of saints shall have discoveries of God through thee" (p. 6). And finally, on Whit Monday 1647, the resolution of this process is revealed to her, as God tells her that "I am about to show thee great things and visions which thou hast been ignorant of" (p. 7): in other words, she is to be a prophet.

This narrative serves as a means of authentication of Trapnel's status as a prophet, a medium for God's word. The signs that marked out a

---

[19] See Dailey, "Sarah Wight"; and Ralph Houlbrooke, "The Puritan Death-bed, *c.* 1560–1660," in *The Culture of English Puritanism, 1560–1700*, ed. Christopher Durston and Jacqueline Eales (New York: St. Martin's Press, 1996), 122–44, here 131–35, 140.

[20] Purkiss, "Producing the Voice, Consuming the Body," 142–43.

prophet — visions, trances, the hearing of voices, the capacity to desist
from food and drink and yet remain healthy — were uncomfortably close
to those that suggested witchcraft, the work of the devil, illness, or madness;[21] indeed, Trapnel anticipates these kinds of objection to her prophecies in *The Cry of a Stone*:

> They say these are convulsion-fits, and sickness, and diseases that
> make thy handmaid to be in weakness. But oh they know not the
> pouring forth of thy spirit, for that makes the body to crumble, and
> weakens nature ...
>
> ... they say, We will not own it to be from God, but from
> some evil spirit, some witchcraft, some design or hiring of men. (pp.
> 29; 73)

Part of the work of *The Cry of a Stone* was to counter these claims con-
vincingly by validating the godliness of its author, the ambiguous signs
that marked her body, and, thereby, the contested utterances that eman-
ated from it. The account of Trapnel's family and early life is an important
element in this, following the conventions of the Puritan conversion
narratives.[22]

There are other features of the text, however, which also suggest an
authenticating function, not least the persistent naming, in the early pages
of the text, of Trapnel's friends and supporters and of the London streets
in which she lived, lodged and moved. Mrs Bond who was then Mrs Kendal, Mrs Smith, Mrs Sansom, Mr Radcliffe, Mr Knollys, Captain Palmer;
Hackney, Aldgate, Southwark, Whitehall, Lime Street, the Minories,
Mark Lane, Blackheath: London is set out before us, and peopled with
characters both notable (Mr Knollys; see p. 86, note 21) and now untrace-
able (Mrs Smith). In so doing, Trapnel maps out a territory for herself, a
territory that is at once the capital of England, the centre of the fast-
moving religio-political manoeuvres of the time, and also, demonstrably,
hers: hers to inhabit, hers to delineate and hers to cite. If, for Fifth Monarchists, the figure of "King Jesus" was the exemplar and guarantor of the
truth of the human/divine encounter, then the New Jerusalem was the
topographical equivalent: the city of Revelation that would exemplify the
perfect coming together of the divine and the social. Indeed, Mary Cary,

---

[21] See Michael MacDonald, *Mystical Bedlam: Madness, Anxiety, and Healing in Seventeenth-
Century England* (Cambridge: Cambridge University Press, 1981); Mack, "Women as Prophets"; Purkiss, "Producing the Voice, Consuming the Body."

[22] For more on the Puritan conversion narrative, see Owen Watkins, *The Puritan Exper-
ience: Studies in Spiritual Autobiography* (London: Routledge and Kegan Paul, 1972); Patricia
Caldwell, *The Puritan Conversion Narrative: The Beginnings of American Expression* (Cambridge:
Cambridge University Press, 1983); Dailey, "Sarah Wight"; Smith, *Perfection Proclaimed*.

another Fifth Monarchist prophet, had published *A New and More Exact Mappe or Description of New Jerusalems Glory* only three years earlier, in 1651, the title of which alone suggests the importance of the spatial as a way of conceptualising God's providence and plan. In the light of this, it becomes significant that the final sentence of *The Cry of a Stone* returns once more to a sense of place in order to underline the trustworthiness of Trapnel's account: "she rose up in the morning, and the same day travelled on foot from Whitehall to Hackney, and back to Mark Lane in London, in health and strength" (p. 79). Place here combines with the condition of the body of the prophet as a joint signifier of godliness: despite fasting ("without any sustenance at all for the first five days, and with only a little toast in small beer once in twenty-four hours for the rest of the time" [p. 79]), she is well enough to walk some twelve miles, and her crisscrossing of London is an irrefutable manifestation of the robustness of her physical condition. The closing words of the text, then, confirm Trapnel's earlier assertion that:

> Father, when thou withdrawest thy glory from thy handmaid, thou shalt leave so much heat as shall refresh the body, and her health shall return again from thee to her, thou wilt give her strength to persevere to the end. (p. 54)

Moreover, the people who dwell in the streets and districts in which Trapnel lives and moves offer the informed reader a network and framework of witnesses, of referees, of testifiers. For readers already sympathetic to Trapnel's message, this catalogue of names ties Trapnel into a godly community, at the same time as references to place ground her in the seat of national government,[23] at ease in its streets and public places, whilst her capacity to traverse the capital marks her body out as "fit" for God's work. Trapnel herself sums up this complicated relationship between place and community, the godly individual's capacity to move amongst them, and the legitimising function of this relationship: "If any desire to be satisfied of it [i.e., her spiritual pedigree], they [her congregation] can give testimony of me, and of my walking[24] in times past" (p. 6).[25]

Trapnel's initial autobiographical account thus works to persuade the doubting reader of the godliness of the ensuing prophetic text which con-

---

[23] Significantly, Trapnel's trance overtakes her in Whitehall, the centre of government.

[24] "Walking" here signifies manner of behaviour or conduct.

[25] Barbara Ritter Dailey notes how Henry Jessey's account of the prophet Sarah Wight's trance of 1647 (*Exceeding Riches* [1658]) also includes lists of notables (including Anna Trapnel) who visited her. See Dailey, "Sarah Wight," 452–54; also Stevie Davies, *Unbridled Spirits: Women of the English Revolution 1640–1660* (London: The Women's Press, 1998), 124–35.

stitutes the greatest part of *The Cry of a Stone*; it does so both by allusion "upward" to the signifiers of godly favour which marked her early life, and by allusion "outward" to her godly contemporaries and the territory they jointly inhabited. In one move, Trapnel claims for herself two spaces that were, in the seventeenth century, typically masculine: that of godly authority and that of public space. Establishing the presence of the former ensures that the latter, Trapnel's "streetwalking," will be read as its concomitant rather than misread as a transgressive feminine refusal of boundaries and constraints.[26] This elision of the divine and the temporal, the religious and the political, is at the centre of seventeenth-century revolutionary discourse, not least that of the radical religious sects such as the Fifth Monarchists. But this example also highlights the instability of all such authorisations: is this the voice of divine prophecy or the voice of the devil? Does Trapnel's "streetwalking" demonstrate the propriety of a concern for God or the waywardness of an unrestrained, unenclosed woman?[27] Does her capacity to flourish without food or drink tell of divine nourishment or diabolic fortification? Do the names she cites convince us of her place within a spiritual community or implicate her, as Needham concludes (see pp. xvii–xviii above), in political conspiracy and insurrection?

Such ambiguities, moreover, could be said to characterise a present-day encounter with *The Cry of a Stone*. Where, for example, are we to locate the text in terms of voice and authorship? This is a text written, for the most part, in the first person: the autobiographical words of Trapnel open

---

[26] Trapnel encountered the issue of femininity and its relationship to boundaries and constraints again in Cornwall later the same year. Arrested and tried for "aspersing the government," she was closely questioned by the magistrates as to why she had travelled to Cornwall. The exchange is noteworthy for the way it deploys differing notions of what would authorise the refusal of geographical constraints:

Lobb: "But why did you come into this country?"
A.T.: "Why might not I come here, as well as into another country?"
Lobb: "But you have no lands, nor livings, nor acquaintance to come to in this country."
A.T.: "What though I had not? I am a single person, and why may I not be with my
        friends anywhere?"
Lobb: "I understand you are not married."
A.T. "Then having no hindrance, why may not I go where I please, if the Lord so will?"

Anna Trapnel, *Report and Plea*, in *Her Own Life: Autobiographical Writings by Seventeenth-Century Englishwomen*, ed. Elspeth Graham, Hilary Hinds, Elaine Hobby and Helen Wilcox (London: Routledge, 1989), 80–81.

[27] Peter Stallybrass notes contemporary links made between the harlot's frequenting of public space and her perceived "linguistic fulness": Peter Stallybrass, "Patriarchal Territories: The Body Enclosed," in *Rewriting the Renaissance: The Discourses of Sexual Difference in Early-Modern Europe*, ed. Margaret W. Ferguson, Maureen Quilligan, and Nancy J. Vickers (Chicago and London: University of Chicago Press, 1986), 123–42, here 127.

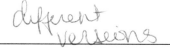

the text proper, followed by her prophetic words. However, this apparently straightforward identification of a first-person voice is complicated by the fact that the prophecy is a transcription of Trapnel's words by a male "relator," a sympathetic member of the crowd. He misses the first three or four days of the prophesying; he does not speak to her directly until the penultimate day of her trance (see p. 66); and his capacity to record her words verbatim was, by his own account, imperfect. He draws attention repeatedly to his omissions, which range from a few words ("The four last words of the last verse are added by the relator, who could not take the maid's own words; her voice as it were dying, and sinking into her breast" [p. 49]) to the utterances of a whole day ("Upon the thirteenth day she uttered many precious things in prayer and songs, which the relator could not for the press of people write down" [p. 38]). Moreover, there is an indication that his transcription is incomplete not only through accident, but also through selection:

> the relator came in and heard her in prayer, wherein she delivered many things, some whereof being of *public nature* were taken, and are presented in the account following. (p. 21; my emphasis)

These details necessarily cause problems for our current preoccupation with the integrity of the original, "authorised," version of a text. Do we retain a sense of the original, spoken, prophecy that was once intact, but which, owing to the circumstances in which the relator wrote, is lost to us, so that the published account is already and necessarily marked, marred, mediated, and incomplete? Or is "the prophecy" in fact no more than the account we find published as *The Cry of a Stone*, the joint product of Trapnel's spoken words and the relator's transcriptions? Does the relator's repeated emphasis on his failure to transcribe comprehensively tell us something important about the manner and circumstances in which the prophecy was uttered, and thus about the prophecy itself? And if we take the published account to be "the prophecy," which of the two extant editions[28] do we take to be the authoritative one? It is not, I suspect, the proliferation of different versions and editions of the prophecy that causes problems for a modern reader, but the search for the location of the original or authentic version. This is not only unlikely ever to be resolved satisfactorily, but also obscures a vital aspect of the circumstances of production of this text, for in effect the prophecy is constituted *cumulatively* by the combination of the spoken prophecy, the attention that this commanded (that is, the crowds that it drew), the status (and possibilities) conferred by the relator's transcription of Trapnel's words, the subsequent

---

[28] For more details of the two extant editions, see the *Textual Note*.

Versions

publishing of an account of this (in *Strange and Wonderful Newes from White-hall*) and then of a fuller edition of the prophecy itself (*The Cry of a Stone*), which was then corrected and republished later the same year. The prophecy could only come into existence by means of precisely this combination of a number of different versions articulated in various locations within a public domain open to verification as "godly'. In other words, the published text cannot finally be separated from its references to the pre-existing spoken version because of its dependence on it for its own validity. The prophecy's "authenticity" lies precisely in its multiplicity, rather than in any single definitive version.

Our desire for textual accuracy is not the only thing called into question by *The Cry of a Stone*; the text also troubles our (post-Romantic) understanding of authorship itself. Not only do we encounter the relator's warnings about the incompleteness of the prophecy as he has recorded it, but we also need to take account of Trapnel's insistence that the words we are reading are not her own, but God's, only mediated through her: "thy servant [i.e., Trapnel] is made a voice, a sound, it is a voice within a voice, another's voice, even thy voice through her" (p. 45). Here, the authorial voice does not seek to establish the truth-value of the text by claiming it to be an authentic expression of the self of the writer; instead, this self, with its worldly predisposition towards vainglory, is a barrier to the acceptability of the text as truth. In so writing, Trapnel is occupying a familiar position within the Christian tradition, deriving from the medieval notion of the author as "auctor," whose authority was based on divine revelation, and whose personality was consequently a matter of indifference.[29] In her own text, of course, Trapnel is *not* a matter of indifference to herself, as she predicts, quite rightly, she will not be to others; she has to struggle to assert her right to disappear from the text, to establish the divine origins of her message in order to disappear as human agent. It is only through a successful denial of the intervention of the self of the author, and the concomitant ascription of authorship to the unassailable authority of God, that the text's reliability can be guaranteed.[30] Significantly, the relator remains nameless throughout; neither his part in the production of this prophecy, nor his personal or spiritual credentials for occupying the position of medium to the medium, figure in any of

---

[29] See Donald E. Pease, "Author," in *Critical Terms for Literary Study*, ed. Frank Lentricchia and Thomas McLaughlin, 2nd ed. (Chicago and London: University of Chicago Press, 1995), 105–17, here 107; Seán Burke, "Changing Conceptions of Authorship," in *Authorship: From Plato to the Postmodern*, ed. Seán Burke (Edinburgh: Edinburgh University Press, 1995), 5–11, here 7.

[30] For a fuller discussion of the issue of authorship in relation to seventeenth-century women's prophetic and autobiographical texts, see Hinds, *God's Englishwomen*, chap. 4.

these processes of authentication. It is he who is the genuinely "selfless" transcriber of the prophetic words; his mark on the text is identifiable only through his shortcomings (his failures to transcribe the spoken discourse comprehensively); in all other senses, he is erased from the text he plays such a large part in producing.

The issues of textual "voice" and of authorship return us to the much-debated question of the relationship between a text and the author's own life: to what extent do we rely on our (perhaps extra-textual) knowledge of the author to make sense of the text? Whilst recent critical discussion of the "autobiographical fallacy" — the reading of a text as a transcription, a translation, a version or an expression of the author's "lived" experiences, or at the very least as symptomatic of his or her character or psyche — has focused primarily on fictional texts, it is clear even from this brief discussion of voice and authorship that this issue is also at stake, albeit rather differently, in such texts as these seventeenth-century autobiographies and prophecies. As non-fictional texts written before the Romantic elision of text and author, and thus with very different discursive constructions of "truth," "author," and "authenticity," we should beware of over-quick recourse to a Barthesian insistence on "the death of the author" as an interpretative device, and the resulting prising apart of author-figure and text; as recent critics of the early modern have demonstrated, the ideas governing the meanings of the "author," and their relationship to their writing, were quite different, and in contestation, at this time.[31] As will be clear from my discussion so far, I have taken account of Trapnel's characterisation of her own early family and spiritual life, and the places in her text which refer "outward" to the geography and the people of contemporary London. These do not, of course, guarantee the unmediated reflection of "the real Anna Trapnel and her world': current critical work has amply demonstrated how prophecy and spiritual autobiography are as much governed by generic conventions and tropes as any other kinds of writing.[32] Instead, I have suggested that they constitute a

---

[31] See Martin Elsky, *Authorizing Words: Speech, Writing, and Print in the English Renaissance* (Ithaca: Cornell University Press, 1989); Pease, "Author"; Margaret W. Ferguson, "Renaissance Concepts of the 'Woman Writer'," in *Women and Literature in Britain 1500–1700*, ed. Helen Wilcox (Cambridge: Cambridge University Press, 1996), 143–68.

[32] See, for example, Caldwell, *Puritan Conversion Narrative*; Dailey, "Sarah Wight"; Purkiss, "Producing the Voice, Consuming the Body"; Sue Wiseman, "Unsilent Instruments and the Devil's Cushions: Authority in Seventeenth-Century Women's Prophetic Discourse," in *New Feminist Discourses: Critical Essays on Theories and Texts*, ed. Isobel Armstrong (London: Routledge, 1992), 176–96; Helen Wilcox, "Private Writing and Public Function: Autobiographical Texts by Renaissance Englishwomen," in *Gloriana's Face: Women, Public and Private, in the English Renaissance*, ed. S. P. Cerasano and Marion Wynne-Davies (Hemel Hempstead: Harvester Wheatsheaf, 1992), 47–62; Kate Chedgzoy, "Female Prophecy in the

significant element in the overall project of the text, in that they are invoked to underline and buttress the truth-claims of the prophecy. By attending to the ways in which texts such as these deploy the life of the author, her movements through the city and the country, her friends and opponents, *as part of* the prophecy rather than incidental to it, we can circumnavigate both the "autobiographical fallacy" with its assumptions of textual reflectionism, and the anachronisms of the "death of the author" premised on Romantic models of authorship. In other words, we can read these elements as telling us about the dynamics of the text rather than about an extra-textual author.

However, there is another, and much simpler, reason why we may wish to take note of and record the biographies of the authors of texts such as these: namely, because the authors, as well as their writings, have all too easily slipped from view in historical and critical accounts of writings from this period. Without the feminist reclamation of their work, they would almost certainly have continued to exist only within the footnotes of these accounts for everyone except the specialist archival researcher. Whilst Trapnel's name circulated widely in 1654, thereafter her fortunes are much harder to trace. We know that in 1655 she returned to Cornwall for a second time, where she was again summoned before local Justices of the Peace, though this time she escaped arrest. Later, in October 1657, she went into an extraordinarily lengthy trance that was to last for some ten months, until August 1658, during which time she stayed in bed and uttered her prophecies in about fifty sessions. These were recorded in *A Voice for the King of Saints* (1658) and in a thousand-page folio with a missing title page, to be found in the Bodleian Library, Oxford. After this, she remained active in sectarian politics; she was attacked in print in 1660, but there are no further reliable reports of her after this.[33] Trapnel's biographical details, then, do have an intrinsic interest for feminist critics and historians, in that they counter the notion that women in earlier centuries were the uniformly downtrodden and passive objects of patriarchal oppression. But they are of interest for other reasons too: their sparsity tells us of the processes whereby women can be written out of history; their juxtaposition within texts with other generic modes helps us to make sense of the dynamics of each component and the relation between

---

Seventeenth Century: The Instance of Anna Trapnel," in *Writing and the English Renaissance*, ed. William Zunder and Suzanne Trill (Harlow: Longman, 1996), 238–54; Suzanne Trill, "Religion and the Construction of Femininity," in *Women and Literature in Britain*, ed. Wilcox, 30–55; Elspeth Graham, "Women's Writing and the Self," in *Women and Literature in Britain*, ed. Wilcox, 209–33.

[33] See *Biographical Dictionary of British Radicals in the Seventeenth Century*, ed. Richard L. Greaves and Robert Zaller, 3 vols. (Brighton: Harvester, 1982–84), 3: 250–51.

the two; and, read alongside other contemporary accounts, they offer a new perspective on the social and cultural context in which Trapnel was writing.

"I SAW IN THE VISION THE ARMY COMING IN SOUTHWARK-WAY": TRAPNEL, FIFTH MONARCHISM, PROPHECY AND HISTORY

Anna Trapnel's texts were not the work of a solitary individual prophesying in a wholly hostile environment; she wrote and spoke from within, and with the support and encouragement of, a community: her fellow Fifth Monarchists, and in particular the congregation of Allhallows the Great in Thames Street, London, which she had joined in 1650. Fifth Monarchism was part of a long tradition of millenarianism,[34] which drew in particular on the prophecies of the books of Daniel and Revelation. Daniel's vision of the successive demise of four corrupt empires — identified as those of Babylon, Assyria, Greece and Rome, the latter extending to the present day in the form of the Roman Catholic Church — were to be succeeded by the fifth and everlasting monarchy, beginning with the Last Judgement and characterised by the establishing of the New Jerusalem, the holy city, on earth, and the personal rule of King Jesus.[35]

It was this moment for which Fifth Monarchists were preparing: Jesus's second coming was expected imminently (some Fifth Monarchists were concerned with trying to establish the date, many settling on 1655 or 1656).[36] Fifth-Monarchist writings were much concerned with this prospect, delineating not only the characteristics of God's kingdom but also its location (ideas of an elect nation, and the fact that England was the only major Protestant state, meant that this was identified as England), and its socio-political composition: the Fifth Monarchist Mary Cary suggested that "kings, and nobles, and mighty men, are to be subjected to his saints," who will seek "the public weal, and safety, and happiness, and salvation of all";[37] moreover, she indicated that the saints would be drawn from all ranks of society: "the time is coming ... when not only men but women

---

[34] On millenarianism, see John A. F. Thomson, *The Later Lollards 1414–1520* (Oxford: Oxford University Press, 1965); Norman Cohn, *The Pursuit of the Millennium: Revolutionary Millenarians and Mystical Anarchists of the Middle Ages*, 3rd ed. (London: Pimlico, 1993); Bernard Capp, *The Fifth Monarchy Men: A Study in Seventeenth-Century English Millenarianism* (London: Faber and Faber, 1972); Bernard Capp, "The Fifth Monarchists and Popular Millenarianism," in *Radical Religion in the English Revolution*, ed. J. F. McGregor and B. Reay (Oxford: Oxford University Press, 1984), 165–89.

[35] Capp, *Fifth Monarchy Men*, 19–35.

[36] Capp, *Fifth Monarchy Men*, 190.

[37] Cary, *New and More Exact Mappe*, 62, 56.

shall prophesy; not only aged men, but young men; not only superiors but inferiors; not only those that have university learning, but those that have it not; even servants and handmaids."[38] Trapnel is even more explicit: Christ, she wrote, "did fulfil his great work" "for to enrich them that/ Before were poor and mean" (p. 41); "the poor, fatherless and widow are the companions of the pure religious ones" (p. 38).

It was in this expectation — that the Fifth Monarchy would arise for the benefit of saints drawn from the marginalised and disenfranchised of society — that the exceptional character of this group lay. Other sects took seriously the prophecies of Daniel and Revelation, and looked toward the establishing of God's kingdom on earth;[39] but it was the Fifth Monarchists who combined these ideas most systematically with an analysis that overtly benefited those who were currently socially, economically and politically dispossessed.[40] Moreover, many Fifth Monarchists sanctioned the use of violence in preparation for this event: from the outset of the movement in 1651, they pledged that anything that stood in the way of God's kingdom "might be utterly pulled down, or brought to nothing";[41] Christ himself, Trapnel tells us, "A soldier . . . will remain / Till all nations are cast" (p. 26). Such statements accounted for much of the fear generated by Fifth Monarchism in the 1650s and 1660s, despite this proving to be a largely rhetorical support for violence, manifested in word rather than in deed. Nor, in fact, was this even a rhetorical stance consistently embraced by all Fifth Monarchists all of the time: in *The Cry of a Stone*, for example, Trapnel acknowledged that "there is a time of the shooting of bullets" (p. 23), but also, addressing the backsliding soldiery, suggested that "if you draw spears against them [the Fifth Monarchists], they will draw nothing but faith and Christ against you, and can you then stand?" (p. 61).

This discrepancy concerning the Fifth Monarchists' attitudes towards violence is indicative of an important caveat for those considering the seventeenth-century sects: namely, the mutability and fluidity of the beliefs and agendas within and between sects, and indeed of the boundaries between one sect and another. During the 1640s and 1650s, radical religious sects proliferated; some — such as the Baptists, the Independents (or Congregationalists) and the Quakers — have endured; others — such as the Familists, the Muggletonians, the Ranters, and the Fifth Monar-

---

[38] Cary, *New and More Exact Mappe*, 238.

[39] Capp, *Fifth Monarchy Men*, 38–45.

[40] Capp, "Fifth Monarchists," 173–76, 185–90.

[41] Christopher Feake, quoted in Capp, *Fifth Monarchy Men*, 59; see also Davies, *Unbridled Spirits*, 158.

chists — have not. Naming these groups is straightforward enough; characterising definitively their boundaries is much less so, for there were continuities between sects, and sometimes controversies within them,[42] that prohibit any absolute delineations. Whilst there were certainly important differences between sects, they also had ideas and concerns in common, such as the inequity of tithes, or the rejection of the notion of a national church.[43] Moreover, over time, as sects rose to prominence and then declined and were superseded by new ones, sectaries moved from one grouping to another, so that the same names are to be found in a variety of different sectarian contexts. Trapnel herself was associated at various times with the Familists, Fifth Monarchists, Baptists and (according to some) Quakers: the print of Trapnel by Gaywood is captioned "Hannah Trapnel, A Quaker and pretended Prophetess."[44]

Perhaps the clearest indication of this lack of absolute distinction between one grouping and another can be seen in the diverse simultaneous allegiances of Fifth Monarchists. Most Fifth-Monarchist groups were established within pre-existing congregations, usually of the Particular Baptists ("particular" because its members subscribed to the Calvinist belief that only an elect, preordained by God, would experience the salvation promised by the second coming of Christ), but also of Independents, and they never entirely separated from these groups. The affiliations of some of the best-known Fifth-Monarchist ministers and teachers exemplify this point: John Simpson, who was lecturer at Allhallows the Great, Trapnel's congregation, was also rector of St Botolph's, Aldgate, "an open-membership congregation of Independents and Baptists";[45] Henry Jessey's congregation was also "open membership," and whilst he himself was a Particular Baptist, he is seen as having more in common with the Independents; Christopher Feake, minister of Christ Church, Newgate and lecturer at St Anne's, Blackfriars, and probably the most prominent and influential of the Fifth-Monarchist leaders at the time The Cry of a Stone was written, was not a Baptist, and was not aligned with any group other than the Fifth Monarchists.

This begs the question of the precise character of the relationship of Fifth Monarchism to these other religious groups. It could be said that Fifth Monarchism was a more overtly political inflection of a widely held

---

[42] See, for example, Susanna Parr's account of her dispute with Lewis Stucley in Her Own Life, ed. Graham et al., 101–45, and Karen L. Edwards, "Susannas Apologie and the Politics of Privity," Literature and History, 3rd ser. 6.1 (1997): 1–6.

[43] See Barry Reay, "Radicalism and Religion in the English Revolution: An Introduction," in Radical Religion in the English Revolution, ed. McGregor and Reay, 1–21, here 14–19.

[44] Reproduced here, frontispiece.

[45] Biographical Dictionary of British Radicals, 3: 176.

set of religious beliefs and practices; Capp suggests that "there was nothing unique in their faith or worship. They differed from the Baptists and the Congregationalists [Independents] only in certain details of eschatology and in their political attitude."[46] Whilst this is a useful characterisation of the different emphases of these groupings, it is also important to bear in mind that such a distinction between religion and politics was a largely meaningless one at this time: all "political" discourse (such as parliamentarian justification of the civil war, Charles I's defence of his actions and position, Cromwell's speeches, or Digger tracts) was articulated in overtly religious terms, and all "religious" discourse (such as Baptist, Quaker or Independent pamphlets, biblical exegesis, or the poetry of Henry Vaughan) had political implications and even agendas. So whilst it helps the contemporary reader to map out these distinctions in the familiar terms of different degrees of religious and/or political commitment, it makes less sense to pursue such distinctions too relentlessly in a seventeenth-century context. More significant here is precisely the *fact* of this elision and of these continuities, crossovers and ruptures, rather than their detail, for they demonstrate so clearly the rapidly shifting religio-political terrain of these years, the formation, dissolution, and reformation of allegiances, partnerships, oppositions, and enmities.

One thing that is clear about the sects in general, however, is the significance of the part that women played in them from the outset, both in terms of numbers and in terms of their activities. Women constituted a large proportion of their congregations: Capp notes (but makes little of) the astonishing fact that "in the [Fifth-Monarchist] church lists which survived, women easily outnumbered men."[47] Women also — to differing degrees, depending on the sect — preached, wrote, published, prophesied, and travelled, testifying to their faith and to their interpretations of current social, religious, and political events and institutions. The sects constituted the arena in which women for the first time erupted into print in large numbers: "Women wrote a greater proportion of the published work than ever before. The breakdown of censorship allowed a wider variety of pubications, and women wrote in increasing numbers after 1640."[48] Prophecies, of which *The Cry of a Stone* was one (though relatively few were as long as this), formed a major part of this output: "well over half the texts published by women between 1649 and 1688 were prophecies."[49] Women's presence in the sects played a part in non-

---

[46] Capp, *Fifth Monarchy Men*, 172.

[47] Capp, *Fifth Monarchy Men*, 82.

[48] Patricia Crawford, *Women and Religion in England 1500–1720* (London and New York: Routledge, 1993), 132.

[49] Hobby, *Virtue of Necessity*, 26. Indeed, whilst all kinds of writings underwent this kind

sectarian responses to these movements, and undoubtedly contributed to
their being judged as irrational, emotional, seditious, disruptive and dis-
orderly: all characteristics associated with women's physiological composition, understood as quite distinct from men's, and constitutive of their
(inferior) femininity.[50] It is imperative, therefore, to think of women not
as an adjunct to the radical sects, but as centrally formative of all aspects
of the sectarian phenomenon: their congregational composition, the writings and prophecies produced from within their ranks, and the ways in
which they were perceived by others.

This discussion of the circumstances of production of *The Cry of a
Stone* (the Fifth-Monarchy movement, prophecy, the importance of women
in the sects) is important not because it offers a *context* for Trapnel's writing — optional, if illuminating, information to enrich the experience of
reading the text — but because it is *directly* productive of the text: its for-
mal characteristics, its focus, its tone, indeed its very existence. I have already discussed the ways in which the text is shot through with references
to Trapnel's contemporaries. More striking even than these, however, are
the repeated references to Cromwell himself. In order to make sense of this
repeated return to Cromwell, and to begin to unravel some of the ways in
which Trapnel's text is bound up with, and structured by, the nuances of
contemporary events, it is worth setting out in brief the main political
events of the months preceding the publication of *The Cry of a Stone*.

In the previous year, in April 1653, Cromwell had, with the backing
of the army, dismissed the Rump of the Long Parliament, which was seen
by many in the army as too slow in introducing reform. It was replaced in
July by a nominated (that is, non-elected) assembly known as the Barebones Parliament or the Parliament of Saints. This assembly marked the
high point of Fifth-Monarchist influence and optimism: it seemed for a
while as if there was a real possibility that the aims of the Fifth Monarchists for an end to tithes and to the national church, for radical law
reform, even for rule by the godly, would be realised, for amongst those
nominated to the assembly were twelve Fifth Monarchists, amongst around
eighty "radicals" (out of a total of 144 MPs), and the whole temper of the
Parliament was, at least at first, characterised by a drive for reform in tune

---

of increase, it is important to bear in mind that this did not significantly alter the *proportion*
of texts published by women. Hobby suggests that women's writings constitute no more than
one per cent of published writings between 1649 and 1688 (*Virtue of Necessity*, 6).

[50] On ideas about women's physiology, see Ian Maclean, *The Renaissance Notion of
Woman: A Study in the Fortunes of Scholasticism and Medical Science in European Intellectual Life*
(Cambridge: Cambridge University Press, 1980); Mack, "Women as Prophets"; Constance
Jordan, *Renaissance Feminism: Literary Texts and Political Models* (Ithaca and London: Cornell
University Press, 1990); Margaret R. Sommerville, *Sex and Subjection: Attitudes to Women in
Early-Modern Society* (London: Arnold, 1995).

with millenarian aspirations. Such optimism was short-lived, however; the moderates within the assembly grew increasingly uncomfortable with the programme of the radicals, Cromwell himself withdrew from his association with them, until in December, barely six months after its inception, the moderates engineered the assembly's dissolution and installed Cromwell as Lord Protector. This, for the Fifth Monarchists, marked the end of the radical experiment of the Commonwealth, as, with the advent of the Protectorate, power was once more invested largely in one man. The anger, frustration and sense of betrayal at this turn of events are apparent in all Fifth-Monarchist writings from this time, and in none more so than *The Cry of a Stone.* Cromwell, the army, the clergy, merchants, the universities: all who were associated with the reinstatement of government by and for the privileged were the targets of Trapnel's wrath.

These events in a very direct sense occasion Trapnel's visionary outpourings in Whitehall (the centre of national government itself) in January 1654: *The Cry of a Stone* is a condemnation of, and a lament for, Cromwell and the army, and their betrayal of the godly cause. Her prophecies speak of the army's entry into London in August 1647 in support of the Independents in Parliament, of the battles of Dunbar (1650) and Worcester (1651), both famous Parliamentarian victories paving the way for the Rule of the Saints, and of the First Dutch War of 1652–54; we hear of Cromwell's illness following the Battle of Dunbar, and his subsequent return to London; she speaks of the general hopes and fears for "the new representative" (the Barebones Parliament), and then of disillusionment with the establishment of the Protectorate. But far from these being set out as chronicles of historical events, we learn of them in accounts of dreams, visions and prophecies, or refracted through the lens of biblical narrative or character. "History" is not seen as sharply distinct from other forms of narrative, whether scriptural or visionary, but of a piece with them, as emblematic and revelatory of God's work in the world and his plans for his people. Once again, Trapnel is not exceptional in this: providentialism was "a language of everyday Puritan belief":[51]

> Providence was the thread of divine purpose which drew together the seemingly disparate events of history ... Divines repeatedly urged the Long Parliament to commission "an History of Providence" which, by placing the events of the 1640s within the divine scheme of history, would become "the Magna Charta of miracles."[52]

---

[51] Blair Worden, "Providence and Politics in Cromwellian England," *Past and Present* 109 (1985): 55–99, here 57.

[52] Worden, "Providence and Politcs," 64; see also Charles Webster, *The Great Instau-*

In *The Cry of a Stone*, as in so many contemporary prophetic (and indeed other) texts, this perspective is manifested in a consistent mingling of history, scripture, personal narrative, prophecy, and interpretative commentary. These identifications and condensations between what we might think of as different discourses are, however, indicative of more than just a sense of God's presence in contemporary political configurations, for they also bear the weight of a host of implications and associations that are likely to be lost to those of us who are not conversant with the biblical narratives in the way that Trapnel's contemporaries were. Trapnel's naming of Cromwell as Gideon (the Old Testament warrior hero chosen by God to free Israel from the occupying force of the Midianites), for example, is the most systematic of these instances of biblical-historical identification: she refers to him in this way on some seven occasions in *The Cry of a Stone*. She writes at first of the two men comparatively ("Oliver Cromwell, then Lord-General, was as that Gideon, going before Israel"), but within a few lines such distinctions are lost, as it became clear to her that "God had provided a Gideon" (p. 9). The moment at which this identification takes place is significant: it is during the Commonwealth army's campaign in Scotland in 1650, occasioned by the Scots' support for the future Charles II, and it relates specifically to the Battle of Dunbar of 3 September 1650, an engagement in which the English were heavily outnumbered by the Scots and yet where, it is said, only twenty English soldiers were killed, as compared with 3,000 of the Scots, another 10,000 of whom were taken prisoner.[53] Trapnel was not alone in interpreting this as a victory contingent upon God's will rather than military skill; Cromwell himself wrote, "We that serve you beg of you not to own us, but God alone; we pray you own His people more and more, for they are the chariots and horsemen of Israel."[54] To take this one step further and identify Cromwell with Gideon might thus be seen as a way of acclaiming the significance of his military prowess and of affirming the godliness of the cause for which he fought. By this account, his fall from grace in Trapnel's eyes, recounted later in the text, would make sense as the military leader overreaches himself in a non-military context, and is consequently left to one side by God; when he benefits from the breakup of the Barebones Parliament by being installed as Lord Protector, Trapnel tells us of her visions of "the deadness of Gideon's spirit to the work of the Lord,

---

ration: Science, Medicine and Reform 1626–1660 (London: Duckworth, 1975), 1–31.

[53] Ian Gentles, *The New Model Army in England, Ireland and Scotland, 1645–1653* (Oxford: Blackwell, 1992), 397–98.

[54] Cromwell, quoted in Austin Woolrych, *Commonwealth to Protectorate* (Oxford: Clarendon Press, 1982), 14. The allusion is to 2 Kings 12.

showing me that he was laid aside, as to any great matters, the Lord having finished the greatest business that he would employ him in" (p. 13).

But there is more to the Cromwell/Gideon nexus than this, for Gideon figured in the seventeenth century for more than his military heroism in fighting a godly war of liberation. He was also noted as a leader who cast out idol worship and reintroduced the true religion to Israel, something that Milton, another writer profoundly shaped by the politics of the English revolution, had planned to explore in a projected play called *Gideon Idoloclastes*; although this project was never realised, Gideon did figure in *Samson Agonistes* as "matchless," "greater than a king."[55] Moreover, just as apposite in relation to Cromwell, and a parallel noted by Andrew Marvell later in the same year in his "First Anniversary," Gideon, when offered the crown in recognition of his military triumphs, refused to become king, on the grounds that it was God alone who ruled over Israel. Other seventeenth-century commentators celebrated Gideon as a hero whose origins were humble,[56] and as a hero triumphing against the military odds.[57] A fiery champion of the true religion, an anti-monarchist, a leader not born to privilege: these facets of the Gideon story inform the identification of Cromwell with the biblical character and help explain Trapnel's insistent return to it through this text. The loss that she was lamenting with his fall from Fifth-Monarchist grace was not just that of a now tarnished military hero, but one who had, as Gideon, condensed so many of their other ideals. Here, she tells us, was someone who was seduced by luxury and flattery, who had taken on the trappings of monarchy.[58] The implication quite clearly is that becoming Lord Protector is tantamount to accepting the crown — the ultimate rejection of the Fifth

---

[55] Christopher Hill, *The English Bible and the Seventeenth-Century English Revolution* (London: Allen Lane/The Penguin Press, 1993), 379.

[56] Hill, *English Bible*, 96, 98.

[57] Worden, "Providence and Politics," 95.

[58] Trapnel was not alone in her assessment of Cromwell's actions as monarchical; many other contemporary commentators came to similar conclusions. These depended not only on Cromwell taking Whitehall (the principal residence of the monarch since the time of James I, and the centre of national government) as his official residence in April 1654, and Hampton Court as his weekend residence (Roy Sherwood, *The Court of Oliver Cromwell* [London, Croom Helm, 1977], 15, 22), but also on a general return to the pomp and ceremony of monarchy, as well as to the "standard symbols of monarchy" in visual and literary representations of Cromwell (Kevin Sharpe, "An Image Doting Rabble: The Failure of Republican Culture in Seventeenth-Century England," in *Refiguring Revolutions: Aesthetics and Politics from the English Revolution to the Romantic Revolution*, ed. Kevin Sharpe and Steven N. Zwicker [Berkeley, Los Angeles, and London: University of California Press, 1998], 25–56, here 47). For an invaluable discussion of the iconography of monarchy that accompanied Cromwell's accession to the position of Lord Protector, see Sharpe, "An Image Doting Rabble."

Monarchy and the rule of King Jesus.) It is not surprising, perhaps, that Trapnel concludes by asking whether Cromwell had not "better to have died in the field, to have fallen in thy tent, than to come into this great palace which the Lord will rent from thee?" (p. 72).

Figuring Cromwell as Gideon, therefore, both condenses and delineates the multiple implications for the Fifth Monarchists of Cromwell's actions. Trapnel could assume that the scripturally highly literate seventeenth-century readership or audience would be fully conversant with the significance of this archetypal biblical character, and read the two men as standing in sometimes metaphorical, sometimes metonymic, sometimes oppositional relation to each other. For those of us approaching the text with a characteristic contemporary unfamiliarity with the Bible, perhaps the best way of working out the dynamics of these strange and unwieldy texts is to turn to the Bible to identify the origins of a character or an allusion, and in this way to piece together the manner in which these might be implicated in the construction of the argument, the rhetoric, or the tone.

"History" thus plays its part in *The Cry of a Stone* in a number of overlapping ways. It features there most obviously in the references to dates, to battles, to political leaders. These are interwoven with biblical references and allusions, so that contemporary history becomes both the fulfilment of God's promises made in the Bible, and a replaying and reworking of a number of the biblical narratives themselves. In its relationship with these (and other) narratives, our attention is drawn to the narrativity of history — history as story — and the ways in which these narratives accrete meaning through the conventionality and familiarity of their narrative development: the godliness of Cromwell's early career, for example, is underwritten by the parallels implicit in his story and Gideon's, whilst his betrayal of the godly cause is confirmed by the deviation of the closure of his own story from the narrative resolution of the Gideon story. "History," then, does not run alongside *The Cry of a Stone* as a context to the text, illuminating but separate; instead, it runs back and forth through the text, in a number of mutually informing manifestations that constitute the distinctive texture and structure of its declamatory autobiographical-prophetic-political-historical-spiritual mode.

"VARIOUS REPORTS GONE ABROAD CONCERNING THIS MAID": THE CRITICAL RECEPTION OF TRAPNEL'S *THE CRY OF A STONE*

Emphasising the embeddedness of *The Cry of a Stone* within the historical moment of its production might lead one to speculate just what the place of such a text is within the context of contemporary literary studies. Does such an emphasis suggest that, after all, this is no more than an obscure historical document, of interest only because of the light it can shed on attitudes within a minor and short-lived millenarian sect of the seventeenth century, telling us nothing about what we generally think of as "seventeenth-century literature"? Until very recently, indeed, we might infer this to have been the dominant critical conclusion; certainly, the clamour of publicity that accompanied Trapnel throughout 1654 has not been matched by scholarly interest in more recent times. In historical writings, her name was, until the last decade or so, to be found only in general discussions of mid-century sectarian activity, whilst in literary-critical or literary-historical accounts, her work did not figure at all.

It is only too easy to rationalise this absence. After all, her writings, like those of so many of her fellow sectaries, were topical, ephemeral, produced within such a specific, short-lived, and ultimately unsuccessful, even inconsequential, religio-political grouping, that any critical attention might seem at best esoteric and at worst perverse. However, other writings with this pedigree have not been so ignored. John Bunyan's spiritual autobiography *Grace Abounding to the Chief of Sinners* (1666) has long had its place in English literary history and criticism; historians have taken account of the writings of male radicals such as Gerrard Winstanley, George Fox and Laurence Clarkson. So the specifically sectarian, political, religious or topical character of the work is not sufficient on its own to account for this scholarly neglect. It seems likely, therefore, that it is the author's gender, together with the perceived lack of "literary" qualities (for literary critics) or the marginality, "extremism" and evanescence of the prophetic mode (for historians) that relegated these writings to the margins.[59]

This is not to say that the critical and historical neglect has been total. The historian Champlin Burrage wrote an article on Trapnel's prophecies in 1911,[60] which, whilst being more descriptive than analytical or evaluative, makes a case for putting these writings on the map. Keith Thomas

---

[59] For a fuller discussion of the marginalisation of these writings, see Hinds, *God's Englishwomen*, chap. 1.

[60] Champlin Burrage, "Anna Trapnel's Prophecies," *English Historical Review* 26 (1911): 526–35.

published an article on "Women and the Civil War Sects" in 1958,[61] and Alfred Cohen one on Trapnel's Fifth-Monarchist contemporary Mary Cary in 1964;[62] whilst neither of these makes specific reference to Trapnel, they begin to make arguments about, on the one hand, the significance of women in the sects in general and, on the other, the contributions of specific women sectaries. Whilst P. G. Rogers's book on the Fifth Monarchists makes little of Trapnel's contribution to the sect, despite noting the sect's "enlightened attitude" towards women,[63] Christopher Hill produced the first fuller consideration of Trapnel's place in the history of mid-seventeenth-century radicalism;[64] and, in the same year, B. S. Capp used Trapnel's texts in what is still the most exhaustive, if misleadingly androcentric (given the compositon of the sect), account of Fifth Monarchism.[65] A decade later, Austin Woolrych offered an account of Trapnel's part in the intricate political manoeuvrings and complicated and shifting allegiances involved in the transition from Commonwealth to Protectorate in 1653.[66] These studies, however, tend to read Trapnel's and other women sectaries' texts as documents indistinct from those produced by men in the sects; only with the 1992 publication of Phyllis Mack's study of women's prophecy in seventeenth-century England,[67] Patricia Crawford's 1993 account of women and religion in England between 1500 and 1720,[68] and Stevie Davies's 1998 energetic celebration of contemporary women's narratives of their activities in the English revolution[69] did we get sustained historical considerations that took account of the specifically gendered character of these prophetic utterances.

Similarly, although Owen Watkins made brief mention of Trapnel in his history of the Puritan conversion narrative,[70] and William York Tindall offered a comparison of Trapnel's spiritual autobiography with Bunyan's,[71] it was not until the expansion of feminist scholarship in the 1980s that sectarian texts began to be more fully discussed within the

---

[61] Keith Thomas, "Women and the Civil War Sects," *Past and Present* 13 (1958): 42–62.

[62] Alfred Cohen, "The Fifth Monarchy Mind: Mary Cary and the Origins of Totalitarianism," *Social Research* 31 (1964): 195–213.

[63] P. G. Rogers, *The Fifth Monarchy Men* (London: Oxford University Press, 1966), 146.

[64] Christopher Hill, *The World Turned Upside Down: Radical Ideas During the English Revolution*, 2nd ed. (Harmondsworth: Penguin, 1975).

[65] Capp, *Fifth Monarchy Men*.

[66] Woolrych, *Commonwealth to Protectorate*.

[67] Mack, *Visionary Women*.

[68] Crawford, *Women and Religion in England*.

[69] Davies, *Unbridled Spirits*.

[70] Watkins, *The Puritan Experience*.

[71] William York Tindall, *John Bunyan, Mechanick Preacher*, Columbia University Studies in English and Comparative Literature (New York: Columbia University Press, 1934), 30–33.

context of literary history and criticism. This context did not, however, mean that critics read these writings in line with what has so often been the initial move in a feminist re-examination of women's writings from the past: namely, their reclamation as examples of the "lost history" of women's writing. From the outset of feminist engagement with this work, critics have rigorously analysed it within its specific generic and historical context.[72] Whilst taking care to eschew any kind of ahistorical claim that these works are "proto-feminist," all take gender to be a formative factor in the texts' production, whether because of the relationship between femininity and prophecy, or because of the social prohibitions concerning women's writing and publishing.[73]

More recently, this feminist work on Trapnel's writings has extended into an exploration of many of the issues that have preoccupied literary criticism in general over the past decade or two. From having been largely ignored in the past as outposts existing beyond the horizon of the critical gaze, Trapnel's writings have increasingly been read as contributing to what have been seen as some of the most pressing literary-critical concerns of the moment. In a time that has seen the conventions and practices of traditional literary study challenged on the one hand for their political underpinnings by Marxist and feminist critics, and on the other hand for their various forms of essentialism and humanism by the theoretical perspectives offered by structuralism and poststructuralism, it is perhaps not surprising that the writings of Trapnel have come to be read in relation to this thoroughgoing scrutiny of "Literature" with a capital L. Critics working on Trapnel's writing have engaged above all with three aspects of these debates: the history and politics of canon-formation; the relationships between gender and genre (specifically, prophecy and autobiography, and the authorisation of the female voice); and textuality, the body and subjectivity.

Sectarian writings such as Trapnel's have proved fruitful for feminist critics interested in the origin and development, and the politics, of the notion of a "literary canon." One influential perspective on this question has been an investigation either of what would now be thought of as "non-literary" genres or of more popular literary forms, in order to assess

---

[72] See, for example, Christina Berg and Philippa Berry, "Spiritual Whoredom: An Essay on Female Prophets in the Seventeenth Century," in *1642: Literature and Power in the Seventeenth Century*, ed. Francis Barker et al. (Colchester: University of Essex Press, 1981), 37–54; Hobby, *Virtue of Necessity*; Purkiss, "Producing the Voice, Consuming the Body"; Wiseman, "Unsilent Instruments"; Chedgzoy, "Female Prophecy"; Trill, "Religion and the Construction of Femininity."

[73] See Hobby, *Virtue of Necessity*, 1–11; Ferguson, "Renaissance Concepts of the 'Woman Writer'."

their changing histories and critical evaluation. Kate Lilley, for example, discusses Trapnel's *The Cry of a Stone*, with its engagement with the terms and character of the New Jerusalem, as an instance of early modern uto-pian writing. This body of writing, she argues, troubles the kinds of gen-eric and evaluative distinction and categorisation on which ideas of "great literature" depend:

> Utopian writing has become a privileged formal and theoretical do-main for feminist women, in ways that explore and frequently erode the distinctions between "primary" and "secondary," "creative" and "critical," "theory" and "practice" ... All utopias are neces-sarily works of theory, of criticism, and of speculative fiction.[74]

Nor is it only classificatory distinctions that are called into question by these texts; it is also the dynamics of literary criticism and the stories con-structed by its scholarship that are challenged. Sue Wiseman argues that:

> The marginalization of seventeenth-century prophetic discourse in relation to the literary canon, and the repeated movement of mar-ginalization in the work of male and feminist scholars, means that the power structures of the seventeenth century appear to be patri-archal, organicist or Hobbesian. But perhaps prophetic discourse offers us a gap in those moments of the grand narrative of the his-tory of political thought ... [W]omen's prophecy undercuts literary history, and some emergent feminist literary histories, by disclosing a concept of authority which is double, treble, multiple and per-petually shifting, disappearing and negotiating.[75]

The critical positioning of sectarian writing such as Trapnel's at the per-iphery of literary history becomes itself the object of study for critics such as Lilley and Wiseman; they do not, however, argue for a simple reposi-tioning of these writings as "key" or exemplary, or indeed as constitutive of a new canon. Instead, a part of their critical agenda is precisely to focus on this marginality in order to identify the premises and processes whereby the texts have been so placed and to consider what kinds of meaning this marginalisation might suggest.

The broad critical focus suggested by this concern for the positioning of these writings in relation to more canonical writings is matched by a detailed set of analytical questions which constitute part of the now long-standing feminist investigation concerning the gendered character of liter-

---

[74] Kate Lilley, "Blazing Worlds: Seventeenth-Century Women's Utopian Writing," in *Women, Texts and Histories 1575–1760* (London: Routledge, 1992), 102–33, here 102–3.
[75] Wiseman, "Unsilent Instruments," 194.

ary genres. Much of the best-known work in this area has concentrated on contemporary examples of particular genres, such as the romance or the family saga,[76] although critical interest in the romance extends to its origins and historical development.[77] Critics of early modern writing, too, have considered the significance of the genres in which women wrote for the proliferation and character of their published discourse. A consideration of sectarian writings is invariably accompanied by, or indeed precipitated by, a sense of the middle years of the seventeenth century constituting some kind of watershed for women's writing. The overall percentage rise of published writing by women is somewhat contested by critics, and the significance of this rise still more so (see p. xxx, note 49); but that there *is* a significance that needs to be debated is not in question. One area that has received a good deal of critical attention has been the importance of the genres of prophecy and spiritual autobiography — the genres which account for the majority of women's published output at this time, and, of course, which constitute Trapnel's oeuvre — in accounting for this increase.

Prophecy is, feminist critics have argued, without question a highly gendered genre in the context of the English Revolution. Prophecy was, during the revolutionary decades of the 1640s and 1650s, a mode of speaking and writing that, along with the radical sects from which it emerged, enjoyed a brief moment of currency and recognition. And, critics have suggested, it was the contemporary status of prophetic discourse that enabled women to emerge in such numbers into the domain of public and political speaking and writing: "the availability of this non-rationalist discursive mode made entry into the domain of politico-religious debate easier for a number of women, whether their contributions to public speech were made within the comparatively narrow confines of a single church or meeting house, or were available and proclaimed within a wider social spectrum."[78]

---

[76] For examples of this kind of work, see Tania Modleski, *Loving With a Vengeance: Mass-Produced Fantasies for Women* (London: Methuen, 1982); Janice Radway, *Reading the Romance: Women, Patriarchy and Popular Literature* (Chapel Hill and London: University of North Carolina Press, 1984); Janet Batsleer, Tony Davies, Rebecca O'Rourke, and Chris Weedon, *Rewriting English: Cultural Politics of Gender and Class* (London: Methuen, 1985); Jean Radford, *The Progress of Romance: The Politics of Popular Fiction* (London: Routledge and Kegan Paul, 1986); Helen Carr, ed., *From My Guy to Sci-Fi: Genre and Women's Writing in the Postmodern World* (London: Pandora, 1989).

[77] J. Paul Hunter, *Before Novels: The Cultural Contexts of Eighteenth-Century English Fiction* (New York: W. W. Norton, 1990); Laurie Langbauer, *Women and Romance: The Consolations of Gender in the English Novel* (Ithaca: Cornell University Press, 1990); Ros Ballaster, *Seductive Forms: Women's Amatory Fiction from 1684 to 1740* (Oxford: Clarendon Press, 1992).

[78] Berg and Berry, "Spiritual Whoredom," 39.

However, it has also been argued that this non-rationalist basis for women's entry into the public domain was at best double-edged and at worst counterproductive, for women's prophetic utterances were legitimated by their reliance on, and reproduction of, a whole range of stereotypes about the "nature" of femininity:

> a woman's right to exercise public authority was not based on the recognition that she possessed qualities of leadership which had previously gone unnoticed. On the contrary, beliefs about the traditional and quite familiar qualities of passivity, irrationality and passion that had formerly justified women's *absence* from the public arena were used to justify their prophetic activities during the Revolution. Women who became publicly active as spiritual leaders had to display evidence of their ecstatic experience. This behaviour might have won them followers, but it also must have reinforced the negative notion that women were irrational and hysterical. The acceptance of women as visionaries, therefore, did not make them any less threatening as figures of authority in the natural order ...[79]

According to Mack, prophecy's reliance on the ecstatic and irrational as its justificatory signifiers left unchallenged the categorisation of femininity as the negative "other" to a rational and dispassionate masculine discourse, an otherness that could, at the Restoration, readily be castigated and demonised with the rest of the "irrational" experiment of the 1640s and 1650s.

If the traits of femininity are regarded by critics as legitimating women's entry into prophetic utterance, these same traits are seen as more problematic with regard to their production of spiritual autobiography.[80] It is not that their *spiritual* significance is necessarily called into doubt — as Elspeth Graham argues, "the very qualities of receptivity, lovingness and emotionality traditionally associated with women, although, in the end, less valuable than masculine rationality, might allow women a recognized spiritual role"[81] — but that the conflict between this spirituality and a proper *social* demeanour comes to the fore. What is seen to be significant in relation to this genre is the negotiation of the social act of

---

[79] Mack, "Women as Prophets," 225.

[80] Note, however, that the genres of prophecy and spiritual autobiography are not sharply separable: *The Cry of a Stone* is itself primarily prophetic, but also has an initial section which follows the conventions and structures of the spiritual autobiography.

[81] Elspeth Graham, "Authority, Resistance and Loss: Gendered Difference in the Writings of John Bunyan and Hannah Allen," in *John Bunyan and his England, 1628–88*, ed. Anne Laurence, W. R. Owens, and Stuart Sim (London and Ronceverte: The Hambledon Press, 1990), 115–30, here 119.

writing and publishing (one typically associated with an unfeminine for-
wardness and immodesty) in such a way as not to compromise the spiritual
credentials of the author. For writers such as Trapnel, whose autobiography is so closely enmeshed with her prophecies, such issues figure minimally: as I have argued earlier in this introduction, the events of her life
bear irrefutable witness to her role as God's handmaid, and the circumstances of their publication, whichever way you look at them, could hardly
be seen as an act of self-will: on the one hand, she uttered them when she
was not herself, or was beside herself, in a trance; and on the other hand,
they were transcribed for publication by an anonymous "relator." Either
way, Trapnel is (within limits) covered as far as charges of vainglory might
be concerned.

What is at stake most obviously in a spiritual autobiography, but in a
different way also in more clearly prophetic writings, is the representation
of the "self" of the author; and this brings me to the third of the current
issues in literary criticism and theory which have been engaged by scholars
through a consideration of Trapnel's writing: namely, subjectivity and, in
particular, the relationship between the body, gender, and subjectivity.

One of the most influential areas of study within early modern scholarship of the last decade and a half, particularly amongst those critics seen
as broadly working with New Historicist, Cultural Materialist, and feminist
agendas, has been an attempt to map the specificities of the changing
sense of what constituted a "self" through the seventeenth century; more
particularly, there has been a focus on the textuality of this self, in the
sense that we necessarily trace its construction through its manifestation
in a variety of cultural genres and forms. Paralleling the New Historicist/
Cultural Materialist deconstruction of the unified *social* self posited by Tillyard,[82] in whose "Elizabethan world picture" all the ranks of society accepted their position within the social hierarchy and together constituted
a harmonious and integrated (*because* hierarchical) social entity, critics
have also challenged the model of the *individual* self proposed by Burckhardt as newly characteristic of the Renaissance.[83] The Burckhardtian
notion of a stable, unified, Renaissance "individual" — a stability and
unity afforded by a conscious sense of a knowable, and implicitly masculine, "inner self" — has been displaced by such critics in favour of a much
more troubled and contingent subjectivity, where the sense of self is subject to, and indeed the outcome of, a whole range of pressures, at times
contradictory and always partial and fragmentary. Far from producing a

---

[82] E. M. W. Tillyard, *The Elizabethan World Picture* (London: Chatto and Windus, 1943).

[83] Jacob Burckhardt, *The Civilization of the Renaissance in Italy*, trans. S. G. C. Middlemore
(London: George G. Harrap and Co., Ltd., 1929).

secure and stable sense of self as *counter* to these pressures, as Buckhardt
had suggested, the argument is that subjectivity itself is, likewise, riven
with conflicts, and is thus always incomplete, fragmented, unstable and
insecure.[84]

Given the radical and fundamental incompleteness of the subject by
this account, the relationship between subjectivity and textuality becomes
clearer: for, if the subject is always contingent and partial, rather than essential and inherent, we can only ever begin to trace its dimensions
through the specifics of its particular manifestations, its discursive constructions. As Roger Pooley argues, "This kind of approach to the 'subject'
(a more appropriate word than the 'self') is much more sensitive to the
multiplicity of roles, the protean nature of the individual, to *self-presen-
tation* more than selfhood."[85] If the self is taken to be presented, or con-
structed, or performed, rather than revealed or described, then the questions that might be asked of it also change: where is that self presented?
From what is it constructed? Before whom is it performed, and on what
occasion, and with what response?

Such questions have been asked and such arguments made through
studies of a whole range of Renaissance writings (though perhaps a dispro-
portionate number of them focus on dramatic texts), but, unsurprisingly,
the proliferation and diversification of autobiographical writing through
the seventeenth century has been seen as peculiarly indicative of the shifting definitions of "the individual" at this time.[86] And if, as Catherine
Belsey has argued, subjectivity "is produced and reproduced in and by a
specific social order and in the interests of specific power-relations,"[87]

---

[84] Stephen Greenblatt, *Renaissance Self-Fashioning: From More to Shakespeare* (Chicago and
London: University of Chicago Press, 1980); Francis Barker, *The Tremulous Private Body* (London: Methuen, 1984); Catherine Belsey, *The Subject of Tragedy: Identity and Difference in Renaissance Drama* (London: Methuen, 1985).

[85] Roger Pooley, "*Grace Abounding* and the New Sense of the Self," in *John Bunyan and
His England*, ed. Laurence et al., 105–14, here 106; my emphasis.

[86] In *Keywords*, Raymond Williams notes how in the seventeenth century, "individual"
meant "indivisible," a sense which signals clearly these associations of homogeneity and unity;
see Raymond Williams, *Keywords: A Vocabulary of Culture and Society* (London: Fontana,
1976), 133–36. For examples of work on early modern notions of "the individual," see Barker,
The Tremulous Private Body (on Pepys and Descartes); Pooley, "*Grace Abounding* and the New
Sense of Self" (on Bunyan); Sidonie Smith, *A Poetics of Women's Autobiography: Marginality
and the Fictions of Self-Representation* (Bloomington, IN: Indiana University Press, 1987) and
Mary G. Mason, "The Other Voice: Autobiographies of Women Writers," in *Life/Lines: Theorizing Women's Autobiography*, ed. Bella Brodzki and Celeste Schenck (Ithaca and London:
Cornell University Press, 1988), 19–44 (on Margaret Cavendish); Wilcox, "Private Writing
and Public Function," and Graham, "Authority, Resistance and Loss" and Graham, "Wom-
en's Writing and the Self" (on women's autobiography).

[87] Belsey, *The Subject of Tragedy*, 223.

then it becomes clear how a feminist analysis, placing in the foreground
the discursive operation of gender, has informed these notions of subjectivity. However, despite this emphasis on the heterogeneity and multiplicity of discourses, and an insistance on listening to the "repressed voices"
of Renaissance culture, the critical emphasis has remained, by and large,
on canonical texts, and in particular on Shakespeare. If we include the
generically very different sectarian writing within this kind of critical gaze,
we can begin to consider how these texts both extend and challenge such
perspectives and arguments. Whilst this work is still in its early stages, it
is already demonstrating its far-reaching critical potential. Sue Wiseman,
for example, has investigated the intersection of gender and subjectivity in
Trapnel's (and other sectarian women writers') work.[88] Trapnel's invoca-
tion of the voice of God in her writing and her denial of any agency as a
self-conscious and autonomous "author" posits a kind of subjectivity that
it is certainly hard to reconcile as unified and coherent: for example, a for-
mulation such as that found on p. 45, "Oh Lord thy servant knows there
is no self in this thing," places Trapnel ("thy servant") in the paradoxical
position of a subject whose act of knowing serves only to erase her as
subject ("self"). As Wiseman put it, "one could say that Anna Trapnel's
work is not recognizable to a humanist feminist critical approach ... because texts by her present us with no unified and gendered subject-position
and no masculine representation of authority short of God."[89] This perhaps suggests yet another explanation of the long-standing critical neglect
of Trapnel and her fellow sectaries: namely, the difficulty, even impossi-
bility, of recuperating these texts and their authors for an essentialist
humanist analysis. For a present-day reader, these sectarian texts remain
"difficult" not only because of the topical references, the complex syntax,
and the density of scriptural allusion, but also because of the unfamiliarity
and intangibility of the subject-position of the first-person "author." Com-
menting on another prophet, writing some twenty years earlier, Lady Eleanor Douglas, Bell, Parfitt and Shepherd note how:

> the "I" of the narrator hardly ever appears. The first-person has
> disappeared completely, and when the writer describes herself it is
> as "her" and "She" ... Her voice as writer is unnamed, unfixed,
> allowing free play between the narrative and prophetic modes and
> accommodating, too, the startlingly practical.[90]

---

[88] Wiseman, "Unsilent Instruments."

[89] Wiseman, "Unsilent Instruments," 198.

[90] *A Biographical Dictionary of English Women Writers 1580–1720*, ed. Maureen Bell,
George Parfitt, and Simon Shepherd (London: Harvester Wheatsheaf, 1990), 253.

The implications of such claims — which could equally well be made of Trapnel's work — are far-reaching. The maintenance of the literary canon, it seems, depends not only on the exclusion of certain texts that are deemed generically or ideologically "inferior," but also of those that trouble too profoundly some of the fundamental premises of the essentialist humanist position (an essential human nature, the primacy of the self-conscious individual, a transhistorical continuity of basic human values) which has been instrumental in the production of this canon.

Another element in this poststructuralist critical concern with subjectivity that has an undoubted relevance to the appraisal of sectarian writings has been the continuing attempt to theorise and problematise the "body," and in particular to think through the relationship between the physical body and "the body politic." Far from the body being seen as a biological constant, a point of stability in the midst of mutable and shifting political manoeuvrings, it is seen instead as an arena of cultural struggle, a place *claimed* by competing discourses as the source and site of an unchanging truth, but which such conflict itself designates as the contrary. "To examine the body's formation," suggests Peter Stallybrass, "is to trace the connections between politeness and politics. But because these connections are never simply given, the body can itself become a site of conflict."[91]

Sectarian writing such as Trapnel's again offers fascinating possibilities for the exploration of such issues. The representation and interpretation of the female body, and particularly the female *prophetic* body, is another factor by means of which critics have begun to interrogate the construction of sectarian subjectivity. Whilst we might expect the female body to belong to the domain of the social and the familial, especially as wife and mother, and therefore be irrelevant (or, indeed an obstacle) to a subjectivity that is predicated on the primacy of the spiritual, it has been argued that, conversely, the body is an important index of the legitimacy of the spiritual/prophetic status that is being claimed by a writer. The capacity of the female body to fast and yet remain healthy, to fall into a trance, to remain unaware of her surroundings and yet to utter godly words, to fall seriously ill and at this moment to be addressed explicitly by God, was (as

---

[91] Stallybrass, "Patriarchal Territories," 123. For other work on the politics of the body in early modern times, see Barker, *The Tremulous Private Body*; Gail Kern Paster, *The Body Embarrassed: Drama and the Disciplines of Shame in Early Modern England* (Ithaca: Cornell University Press, 1993); Jonathan Sawday, *The Body Emblazoned: Dissection and the Human Body in Renaissance Culture* (London and New York, Routledge, 1995); Valerie Traub, "Gendering Mortality in Early Modern Anatomies," in *Feminist Readings of Early Modern Culture: Emerging Subjects*, ed. Valerie Traub, M. Lindsay Kaplan, and Dympna Callaghan (Cambridge: Cambridge University Press, 1996), 44–92.

I suggested earlier) read as a marker of the legitimacy of the author's claim
to be a prophet; the very visibility of these bodily signs, argues Purkiss,
"was a means by which she negotiated a space to speak within the constraints of seventeenth-century religious discourse."[92] However, the importance of the body as a marker of the legitimacy of prophetic discourse
is accompanied by an insistence on the body as a barrier to, or a necessary
casualty of, the attainment of the condition of "prophet"; as Trapnel puts
it:

> Vision! The body crumbles before it, and becomes weak: men are
> mistaken when they think that the great things of God will puff up;
> no, the more thou givest of thyself, the more they are humbled;
> they that have the flowings of thee, are self-denying . . . (p. 77)

Such a dissolution of the body and the self, Trapnel makes clear, is to be
sought, as an index of the subject's relationship with the divine: "Lord,
give me an humble, broken, melting frame of spirit, put upon me a spirit
of prayer and supplication" (p. 11). The paradox of the attainment of the
state of spiritual grace being dependent on a loss of subjectivity is of course
in many ways a conventional biblical one (see, for example, 1 Corinthians
1:28). It does, nonetheless, result in a strangely disjunctive representation
of the prophetic body as both the absolute guarantee of spiritual legitimacy
and, simultaneously, a carnal impediment whose dissolution serves also as
a guarantee of such legitimacy. By this account, the female prophetic body
could hardly be further from a transhistorical biological "given"; instead,
its manifestations, representations, behaviours, and meanings are as po-
lemical and as open to contestation as any other element of Trapnel's
text. Hence, Trapnel's note of the "continual fullness in my stomach" (p.
8) during her period of visionary fasting is less a reassurance concerning
her physical wellbeing and more an assertion of her spiritual health.

A survey of critical responses to Trapnel's work is, inevitably at this
stage, largely a matter of raising questions and sketching out ways in
which existing critical preoccupations are starting to be brought to bear on
new kinds of hitherto undertheorised writing. That this is the case is precisely why a new edition of Trapnel's work is so timely. *The Cry of a Stone*
has not been republished since 1654. Whilst we might lament the continuing focus on canonical works, as long as these remain the only readily
available examples of Renaissance and early modern writing, then any
challenge to the canonical object of study is likely to remain, at a practical
level, a marginal and minority critical activity. Until we have new edi-

---

[92] Purkiss, "Producing the Voice, Consuming the Body," 141; see also Smith, *Perfection Proclaimed*, 49–53.

tions of texts such as *The Cry of a Stone*, we will never get beyond the "beginnings" of this kind of work. Perhaps, at last, with their republication, not only will these texts begin to make their mark on existing areas of critical debate, but also their own specificities, styles, and strategies might begin to suggest new areas of investigation. It is in that hope that this new edition of Trapnel's text has been prepared.

TEXTUAL NOTE

The copy-text for this edition is from Cambridge University Library, shelf-mark Syn.7.65.157. It has been compared with the copy held in the British Library, shelfmark E730 (3). These two texts are referred to throughout this edition as "CUL" and "BL" respectively.

After comparing these two copies,[1] I have concluded that the British Library copy (BL), though published in the same year as the Cambridge University Library copy (CUL), is a different edition. The majority of the type is set differently in BL, line lengths and size of type differing between the two copies; signatures differ; printers' ornaments on page 1 are different, as are the illuminated initial letters. Nonetheless, both editions conclude on page 76.

Certain corrections and "improvements" to BL suggest that it is a later edition than CUL: the verse in BL has mostly been set out in stanzas rather than in continuous format as in CUL (perhaps in order to emphasise the "poetic" nature of Trapnel's spontaneous prophesying); certain lines and words have been added to BL; and the order of certain words in the verse has been inverted; these differences are footnoted. Because it appears to be the first edition, CUL has been taken as the copy-text here.

CUL and BL represent the only two distinct editions of the text. Sample pages from all other extant copies of the text have been obtained, and all are from either the first (CUL) or second (BL) edition. Whilst these copies have been identified as being of one or other of these two editions, variants within these editions have not been checked.

---

[1] I am indebted to Maureen Bell of the University of Birmingham for her invaluable and expert help with the comparison of the two copies of the text.

Locations of the Two Editions

The Cry of a Stone (1654): First Edition (CUL)	*The Cry of a Stone* (1654): Second Edition (BL)

Cambridge University Library, Shelfmark Syn.7.65.157. Copytext for this edition.

University of Chicago, USA

Edinburgh University, Scotland

Harvard University, USA

British Library, Shelfmark E730 (3). Compared with CUL for this edition, and differences footnoted.

Bodleian Library, Oxford, UK

Clark Memorial Library, University of California, Los Angeles, USA

Earlham College, USA

Friends Library, London, UK

Folger Shakespeare Library, USA

Haverford College, USA

Huntington Library, USA

Lampeter, University of Wales

University of Minnesota, USA

Swarthmore College, USA

Worcester College, Oxford, UK

EDITORIAL NOTE

In this edition the following editorial practice has been followed:

1. The corrections and additions from BL have been added to CUL, footnoted. Differences in spelling have not been noted.
2. Spelling has been modernised, except when to have done so would have resulted in a marked change in pronunciation.
3. Italicisation has been removed where it indicated proper nouns, and quotation marks have been substituted for it where it indicated quotation or reported speech. Quotation marks have also been used where direct speech is clearly indicated, principally in the first section (the autobiographical account) of *The Cry of a Stone*. They have not been introduced into the prophecy taken down by the relator, as, unsurprisingly (given the genesis of the text), it is often unclear when the quotation ends and Trapnel's prophetic voice takes over again. In these instances, a capital letter is used to mark the beginning of the quoted material: for example, "Oh, say they, We thought it had been by this time ..." (p. 35).
4. Punctuation has been changed minimally. No attempt has been made to render the writing "grammatically correct" in the current sense, but, conversely, practices have not been retained that might render the text either quaint or confusing for a modern reader: for example, I have substituted full stops for colons and semi-colons where they were used to conclude a sentence, and possessive apostrophes have been inserted. Capital letters have been retained only for proper nouns, and removed where used for common nouns. They have been retained where a metaphorical reference is being made to God or Christ as King, General, Protector, Conservator, et cetera, in order to clarify the association.
5. Editorial identifications of biblical references, allusions and echoes in the text are included in square brackets. Those biblical references that are not in square brackets are Trapnel's own.

The Cry of a Stone[1]

or a

relation

of

something spoken in Whitehall,

by Anna Trapnel, being in

the visions of God.

Relating

to the Governors, Army, Churches,

Ministry, Universities, and

the whole Nation.

Uttered

in prayers and spiritual songs, by an

inspiration extraordinary, and full of wonder

in the eleventh month, called January, 1653[2]

London, printed 1654

To all the wise virgins in Sion, who are for the work of the day, and wait for the bridegroom's coming.[3]

It is hoped in this day, a day of the power of God, a day of wonders, of shaking the heavens and the earth [Haggai 2.6], and of general expectation of the approachings of the Lord to his temple, that anything that pretends[4] to be a witness, a voice, or a message from God to this nation, shall not be held unworthy the hearing and consideration of any, because it is administered by a simple and unlikely hand. Far be that from us, who have seen the foolish things of the world to confound the wise [1 Corinthians 1.27], babes and children to bring to nothing the scribes[5] and disputers of this world, the first to be last, and the last first [Matthew 19.30, 20.16; Mark 10.31; Luke 13.30]; far be it from us, who are and shall yet be named the valley of vision [Isaiah 22.1,5], to bind up the goings forth of the most free and eternal spirit at any time, especially in these last days, within any law, custom, order or qualification of man, how ancient or accustomed soever, or within any compass narrower than the promise itself, John 7.37, who may bind where God hath loosed? Canst thou bind the sweet influences of the Pleiades, or loose the bands of Orion [Job 38.31]? He openeth, and no man shutteth [Revelation 3.7]. And let it be considered, if upon this stumbling-stone of the spirit's freedom, the wise and learned ones, both in the days of Christ and of the apostles, and in our days, have not stumbled and fallen, and been broken to pieces.

Two things are foretold by all the prophets, shall be brought to pass, which seal up the prophesies, and finish the mystery of God: the Lord's appearing in his glory upon Mount Sion [Isaiah 24.23; Joel 2.32; Obadiah 17, 21; Micah 4.7; Revelation 14.1]; and the darkening of sun and moon [Isaiah 24.23; Joel 2.10, 3.15; Matthew 24.29; Mark 13.24; Luke 23.45], that is, the shaming, confounding and casting out of all wisdom and power, and whatsoever is but the excellency and glory of man. Now if we see these high and precious effects beginning to put forth either in sons or daughters, in handmaids or servants, let us rejoice and be glad, for the summer is nigh at hand [Matthew 24.32; Mark 13.28; Luke 21.30]. It was the desire of this maid to present this her testimony to you, though it is not for you only, but for all.

If any may be offended at her songs, of such it is demanded if they know what it is to be filled with the spirit, to be in the mount with God [2 Peter 2.18], to be gathered up into the visions of God, then may they judge her; until then, let them wait in silence, and not judge in a matter that is above them.

There being various reports gone abroad concerning this maid, too many being such as were not according to truth, whereby it comes to pass that the things she spake do not appear to men as they came from her, but as deformed and disguised with the pervertings and depravings of the reporters; therefore it was upon the heart of some that heard her (as judging it might be a service done to many, hurt to none but such as fear the light) to present to public view a true and faithful relation of so much as for some seven or eight days could be taken from her by a very slow and unready hand, whereby a fair opportunity is laid before offended and unsatisfied spirits to examine, try and judge, and happily to correct their censures. And also the things herein related may come to the knowledge and reach the hand of them whom they especially concern, if so be they will in meekness search and enquire, whether it be the Lord that hath spoken to them in it.

Upon the seventh day of the eleventh month,[6] called January, 1653, being the sixth day of the week, Mr Powell,[7] preacher of the gospel in Wales, being according to order from the council now sitting in Whitehall[8] come thither to give an account before them of some things by him delivered in his public exercises in London, among other friends who came thither to see what would be done with him, there came a maid, Mrs Anna Trapnel by name. Who, waiting in a little room near the council, where was a fire, for Mr Powell's coming forth, then with a purpose to return home, she was beyond and besides her thoughts or intentions, having much trouble in her heart, and being seized upon by the Lord, she was carried forth in a spirit of prayer and singing, from noon till night, and went down into Mr Roberts'[9] lodging, who keeps the ordinary[10] in Whitehall. And finding her natural strength going from her, she took her bed at eleven o'clock in the night, where she lay from that day, being the seventh day of the month, to the nineteenth day of the same month, in all twelve days together; the first five days neither eating nor drinking anything more or less, and the rest of the time once in twenty-four hours, sometimes ate a very little toast in small beer, sometimes only chewed it, and took down the moisture only, sometimes drank of the small beer, and sometimes only washed her mouth therewith, and cast it out. Lying in bed with her eyes shut, her hands fixed, seldom seen to move, she delivered in that time many and various things; speaking every day, sometimes two, three, four and five hours together; and that sometimes once a day, and sometimes oftner, sometimes in the day only, and sometimes both in the day and night. She uttered all in prayer and spiritual songs [Ephesians 5.19; Colossians 3.16] for the most part, in the ears of very many persons of all sorts and degrees, who hearing the report, came where she lay; among others that came, were Colonel Sydenham, a member of the council, Colonel West, Mr Chetwood, Colonel Bennett, with his wife, Colonel Bingham, Captain Langdon, members of the late parliament; Mr Courtney, Mr. Birkenhead,[11] and Captain Bawtrey,[12] Mr Lee,[13] Mr Feake the minister,[14] Lady Darcy, and Lady Vermuyden,[15] with many more who might be named. The things she delivered during this time were many; of the four first days no account can be given, there being none that noted down what was spoken. For the rest of the time, from the fifth day to the last, some taste is herein presented of the things that were spoken, as they could be taken by a slow and imperfect hand.

And to hold out all just and full satisfaction to those questions, scruples or demands, which a relation of this nature is apt to beget, touching the condition of the party, where or what she is; to whom is she known? Is she under ordinances? What hath been her conversation formerly? etc., before you come to the relation itself, here is first offered to you an account of the party's condition in her relations, her acquaintance, her conversation, the dispensations of the Lord to her in clouds and bitter storms of temptations, in manifestations of light and love, in visions and revelations of things to come; all this is presented to you in the following narration, taken from her own mouth.

I am Anna Trapnel, the daughter of William Trapnel, shipwright, who lived in Poplar, in Stepney parish; my father and mother living and dying in the profession of the Lord Jesus. My mother died nine years ago, the last words she uttered upon her death-bed, were these to the Lord for her daughter: "Lord! Double thy spirit upon my child." These words she uttered with much eagerness three times, and spoke no more. I was trained up to my book and writing,[16] I have walked in fellowship with the church-meeting at Allhallows (whereof Mr John Simpson is a member)[17] for the space of about four years; I am well known to him and that whole society, also to Mr Greenhill, preacher at Stepney,[18] and most of that society, to Mr Henry Jessey,[19] and most of his society, to Mr Venning, preacher at Olaves in Southwark,[20] and most of his society, to Mr Knollys,[21] and most of his society, who have knowledge of me, and of my conversation. If any desire to be satisfied of it, they can give testimony of me, and of my walking in times past.

Seven years ago I being visited with a fever, given over by all for dead, the Lord then gave me faith to believe from that scripture, "After two days I will revive thee, the third day I will raise thee up, and thou shalt live in my sight" [Hosea 6.2]; which two days were two weeks that I should lie in that fever, and that very time that it took me, that very hour it should leave me [John 4.52–53], and I should rise and walk, which was accordingly. From this time, for a whole year after, the Lord made use of me for the refreshing of afflicted and tempted ones, inwardly and outwardly. And when that time was ended, I being in my chamber, desired of the Lord to tell me whether I had done that which was of and from himself. Reply was, "Thou shalt approve thy heart to God, and in that thou hast been faithful in a little [Matthew 25.21,23], I will make thee an instrument of much more; for particular souls shall not only have benefit by thee, but the universality of saints shall have discoveries of God through thee." So upon this I prayed that I might be led by the still waters [Psalm

23.2], and honour God secretly, being conscious to myself of my own evil heart, looking upon myself as the worst of all God's flock; the Lord upon it told me that he would out of the mouth of babes and sucklings perfect his praise [Matthew 21.16]; then I remained silent, waiting with prayer and fasting, with many tears before the Lord for whole Sion. And upon that day called Whitsun Monday, which was suddenly after, I finding my heart in a very low dead frame, much contention and crookedness working in my spirit, I asked of God what was the matter; he answered me thus: "I let thee see what thou art in thyself to keep thee humble, I am about to show thee great things and visions which thou hast been ignorant of"; I being thus drawn into my chamber. After this there was a day of thanksgiving that I kept with the church of Allhallows in Lime Street,[22] for the army that was then drawing up towards the city,[23] in which I had a little discovery of the presence of the Lord with them, in which day I had a glorious vision of the New Jerusalem, which melted me into rivers of tears, that I shrunk down in the room; and cried out in my heart, "Lord, what is this?" It was answered me, "A discovery of the glorious state of whole Sion, in the reign of the Lord Jesus, in the midst of them, and of it thou shalt have more visions hereafter." So then when the day was ended, I retired to my chamber, at that time living in the Minories in Aldgate parish,[24] where I conversed with God by prayer, and reading of the scriptures, which were excellently opened to me touching the proceedings of the army.

It was first said to me that they were drawing up toward the city (I not knowing anything of it before) and that there was a great hubbub in the city, the shops commanded to be shut up. Upon this I went down, and enquired of the maid of the house whether there was any stir in the city. She answered me, "You confine yourself to your chamber, and take no notice of what is done abroad. We are commanded," said she, "to shut up our shops, and there are great fears amongst the citizens; what will be the issue, they know not." With that I answered, "Blessed be the Lord that hath made it known to so low a servant as I"; then repairing to my chamber again, I looked out at the window, where I saw a flag, at the end of the street. This word I had presently upon it, "Thou seest that flag, the flag of defiance is with the army, the King of Salem[25] is on their side, he marcheth before them, he is the captain of their salvation." At the other end of the street, I, looking, saw a hill (it was Blackheath); it was said to me, "Thou seest that hill, not one but many hills rising up against Hermon Hill,[26] they shall fall down and become valleys before it." It was then said unto me, "Go into the city, and see what is done there" [Acts 9.6]; where I saw various things from the Lord in order to his appearance with the army. As I was going, hearing of a trumpeter say to a citizen these words: "We have many consultations about our coming up, but nothing yet goes on"; presently it was said to me, ("The counsels of men shall fall, but the counsel of the Lord stands sure, and his works shall prosper.") So repairing home, I had many visions, that the Lord was doing great things for this nation. *many prophets see this*

And having fasted nine days, nothing coming within my lips, I had upon the ninth day, this vision of horns:[27] first I saw in the vision the army coming in Southwark-way,[28] marching through the city with a great deal of silence and quietness, and that there should be little or no blood spilt; this was some weeks before their coming in.

Then broke forth another vision as to the horns; I saw four horns, which were four powers, the first was that of the bishops, that I saw was broken in two and thrown aside; the second horn more white, had joined to it an head, endeavouring to get up a mount, and suddenly it was pushed down, and broken to pieces; the third horn had many splinters joined to it, like to the scales upon the back of a fish, and this was presented to be a power or a representative consisting of many men, having fair pretences of love to all under all forms; this I saw broken and scattered, that not as much as any bit of it was left. As to the fourth horn, that was short, but full of variety of colours, sparkling red and white; it was said to me, "This is different from the three other, because great swelling words and great offers of kindness should go forth to all people from it, like unto that of Absalom, speaking good words to the people in the gate to draw them from honest David."[29]

I was judged by divers friends to be under a temptation, as H. J. and Jo. S.,[30] to be under a temptation for not eating. I took that scripture, "Neglect not the body" [Colossians 2.23], and went to the Lord and enquired whether I had been so, or had any self-end in it to be singular beyond what was meet. It was answered me, "No, for thou shalt every way be supplied in body and spirit," and I found a continual fullness in my stomach, and the taste of divers sweetmeats and delicious food therein, which satisfied me, that I waited to see the issue, which was exceedingly to be admired; I remaining ever since in much health.

Some years after, when the army was designing a war with Scotland,[31] I was dissatisfied, judging many that were godly in those parts might be cut off ignorantly; and upon this I sought the Lord, and the Lord after prayer directed me to the 9th of Zecchariah, verse 11:[32] "The eyes of the Lord shall be seen over them, and his arrow shall go forth as the lightning, the Lord God shall blow the trumpet, and shall go through with the whirlwinds of the south." The Lord said that his eye, not only his all-seeing eye which runs to and fro through the earth, but an eye of grace and love to them as his peculiar treasure, was over them of the army, and not only so, but they should see it. And as to his arrow, it was that sharp dealing of his with the enemy; as to the lightning, it was those burning devourings of those several places that should be ruinated by the army in those parts; and as to the trumpet, that the Lord would show forth a mighty alarm to his people, before whom many high and great ones of the Scots should tumble down, and that he had raised up a Gideon,[33] bringing that of Judges 7 to me, to prove Oliver Cromwell, then Lord-General, was as that Gideon, going before Israel, blowing the trumpet of courage and valour, the rest with him sounding forth their courage also; that as sure as the enemy fell when Gideon and his army blew their trumpets [Judges 7.16–22], so surely should the Scots throughout Scotland be ruinated. Upon this I praised for some hours together, that God had provided a Gideon, and this I saw both by vision, and faith, and prayer and praises, that God had appointed him for the work of that present day to serve this nation; and told me that great things should be done, and that he should take his circuit through Scotland, and the enemy should draw near to us, even to the gates of the city, and there be defeated.

So I remained praying, keeping many fasting days in my chamber, till six weeks before Dunbar fight;[34] and then I had visions given me concerning that first overthrow of the Scots, where I saw myself in the fields, and beheld our army, and their general, and hearing this voice, saying, "Behold Gideon and the lapping ones with him!"[35] With that I was much taken, that they were likened unto that old Gideon and his company. And then I saw them in a very ill posture for war, and much dismayed, looking with pale countenances, as if affrighted at the multitude of the Scots that were come out against them; whom I saw at a little distance from them, the light of the sky being over their heads, which prompted them the more to the battle, seeing our army with darkness over them and much disheartened. And they thinking that our army was running away, they marched up with very great fury against them, and suddenly as our army turned, who seemed but a little while to stand before them, the light of the sky being drawn from the Scots to our army, they were encouraged and immediately I saw the Scots fall down before them, and a marvellous voice of praise I heard in our army. Then was I taken weak in my outward man,[36] keeping my bed fourteen days, neither drinking nor eating but a draught of small beer, and a bit of toast once in twenty-four hours; and as soon as this vision was over, I broke forth to the singing of their deliverance in Scotland; in which time many resorted to me of them that were for the Presbyterian Government, viz. Dr French's wife, Mrs Bond, who was then Mrs Kendal, Mrs Smith, who all lived in Hackney, and Mrs Sansom of Tower-hill,[37] and they related this vision to Mr Ash[38] the minister, who waited till they saw it accomplished, and then admired.

Upon the fifth of November last save one, 1652, the Lord brought that scripture to me, "Who is a God like unto thee, glorious in holiness, fearful in praises, working wonders?" [Exodus 15.11], from which the Lord showed me that his glory and praise, and wonders he was bringing forth as upon the land, so now upon the seas. And the Lord again showed me in a vision, that many men of account should be taken away in the first great battle;[39] and I lay in this vision from the first day of the week at night, until the second day at night, and stirred not, nor spoke, but sometimes sang of a great victory that I saw upon the seas, ships burning, bones and flesh sticking upon the sides of the ships, the sails battered, and the masts broken, and many such dreadful things as to the Hollander. Seeing many godly friends also dropping into the sea, and their bodies beaten in pieces, it remained a long while to my view, but the victory that I saw in the conclusion, produced many songs, crying out, "Oh, who is a God like unto thee? According as thou saidst thou wouldst be, so Lord I see thee." At this time, I keeping of my bed seven whole days and eight nights in Mark Lane, at Widow Smith's, glazier,[40] where were many spectators of account, both sea-captains and others: Mr Allen, a Common Councilman, Mr Smith, Mr Radcliffe, Captain Palmer, Mr Knollys,[41] and several other men of account in the city; at this time for seventeen days I ate nothing but two broiled herrings, and drunk water and small beer.

Two months after this, in the twelfth month, called February, 1653, the Lord suffered Satan to buffet me, yet I questioned not the truth of any of my visions and revelations, but said, "If I shall be thrown into hell, yet they were the truths of the Lord God, and should certainly come to pass." But I remained in grievous bitterness, being hurried by Satan, and he prevailing over me in a very high nature, moving me to blaspheme; but the Lord kept me from uttering any such thing, though I was tortured in my body, as if he had the full possession thereof, and being persuaded that he had power over my body, and natural life, to make an end of it, though I believed from the seal[42] that I had had eight years before, that I should be saved through the fire. This temptation remained with me from the first of the twelfth month, 1653, till the latter end of the second month, called April,[43] lying in the Minories seven days, in which time I had two godly men and a godly woman watched with me every night, temptations of all sorts were so violent upon me. And at the end of those seven days, my body was freed from that torture caused by Satan, and I repaired home to Hackney, to my kinsman's house, Mr Wythe,[44] and there I remained till the latter end of April, under very bitter storms, being forced by Satan to walk up and down the fields, attempting to throw myself into a well, saying, "God shall not be dishonoured." "For it shall be thought," said Satan, "some put thee in, and so thou shalt be in happiness presently; for what can pluck thee out of thy Father's hand, he hath made an everlasting covenant with thee, ordered in all things, and sure, and this is all thy desire, and all thy salvation, which thou hast made mention of to many." And I was forced to lie in ditches frequently, till it was dark night, that some found me, and led me home. And again frequently I took knives to bed with me, to destroy myself and still they were snatched out of my hand, I know not how, not by any creature. I durst not eat nor drink for four days together, because it was said to me, "If thou dost, thou worshippest the devil. For in everything give thanks, whether thou eatest or drinkest, do it all to the glory of God [1 Corinthians 10.31]; but thou canst do nothing to the glory of God, therefore thou gratifiest Satan; and do not add sin to sin by so doing." In this time still Satan came as an angel of light [2 Corinthians 11.14], though I was so full of terror, he still affrighted me in everything. If I did so and so, I should sin, that I durst not speak to any that feared the Lord, nor I durst not have any prayer, because, he said, I sinned if I prayed, or suffered any to pray for me; and I was exceeding afraid to sin, though he drew me abundantly by his false pretences to vow against coming ever among the saints, or into institutions more. And said to me also that if I did, I were the most notorious liar that ever spake, and that made me afraid, because of that dreadful scripture in the last of the Revelation where the fearful are ranked with those that shall have their portion in the lake [Revelation 21.8]. Many other dreadful assaults I had, and casting myself at length down on the ground, said, "Lord there is no recovery, I shall surely go out like a snuff." Presently, there shone a light round about me, and this saying: "Arise, why liest thou upon thy face, pray and eat, this day is salvation come to thy house, behold, this is the day of salvation, this is the acceptable time [2 Corinthians 6.2; Isaiah 49,8]. Ask now what thou wilt in the height or in the depth, and see whether God will not give thee the desire of thy soul." I replied and said I would not tempt the Lord; he answered me it is not a tempting of God when he requires this of thee. I said then, "Lord, give me an humble, broken, melting frame of spirit, pour upon me a spirit of prayer and supplication," which immediately the Lord did in abundant measure, and many singings concerning the excellent nature of faith. And now having procured a very terrible ague and fever upon my body, in locking myself up in such bitter cold weather, coming at no fire, nor among any, lest they should speak to me of my former experiences, which I found did aggravate my sorrow very much; but the Lord as he had cured me in my spirit, so by faith he restored my body. And as to that temptation mentioned, never to come among the saints again, which was that grand temptation that drew in the other, it being first settled in my heart, I desired that the Lord would give me a scripture to inform me that this was slain and should no more have the least puttings forth in me. At which time opening my Bible this was given me in Job: "Thou hast been tied in fetters and holden in chains of affliction, and it is that the Lord might show thee thy work and thy transgression which hath exceeded in this time of thy assaults. Now he openeth thine ear to discipline, and he commandeth that thou return from iniquity" [Job 36.8–10]. "Lord," said I, "What is my work?" Reply was to go forth to the tempted, and whatever their temptations were, I should have to speak forth to them. And also he having opened mine ear to discipline, I should go among the saints, and that company that I walked in fellowship with, and there I should manifest a departing from that iniquity that Satan had led me into, in drawing me from all institutions, making me believe that I should find the presence of God in reading and praying, and in the Book of the Creature,[45] and that should satisfy me; but I found him a liar to purpose, though he told me that God had dealt all along singularly with me. And though I were not to forsake the assemblies of the saints, yet if God would deal in a singular way with me, it should not go upon my account, but the Lord might do what he pleased. And so he endeavoured to bring me into those Familistical ranting tenents,[46] that I had almost spent my lungs in pleading against. The Lord having thus freed me, he hath kept this upon my heart to beg the life of faith and self-denial, to hold forth these his dispensations towards me both in Gath and Ashkelon,[47] whom he bid me tell them unto.

After my storms, I went down into the country, to Hillingdon, near to Uxbridge, and so soon as I came thither, at one Mr William Atcroft's house, the Lord filled me with many spiritual hymns, as to my temptations, promising me that my joy should abundantly outpass my sorrow. And while I was thus singing and triumphing over Satan, challenging now a battle, and seeing the Lord so glorious before me, I was drawn into my visions, as the calling in of the Jews,[48] the overthrowing and shaking all nations. And a vision I had concerning the dissolution of the Parliament,[49] about four days before it was, not knowing anything of that nature was intended, which I sung; the manner of it, that suddenly Gideon (as I called him) and M.G. Harrison[50] came into the Parliament-house and desired removal of them, desiring Mr Speaker[51] to deliver up his commission, and so I saw suddenly a departure of them, though they were very loath thereunto. And this many in the country can witness, the minister of Hillingdon, Mr Taverner[52] by name, whose wife sent word of it within four days after I had the vision of it: in these visions I lay seven days, and then arose having strength as formerly.

Nine weeks after this, coming up to London, Mr Smith, a linen-draper[53] in Newgate market at the Golden Anchor, asked me what I thought of this new representative[54] that was then in choice. I answered that I had faith to believe that little good should be done to the nation by their sitting.

So after this I had divers visions at times, wherein I saw their breaking up; I lying frequently, sometimes ten days together, sometimes seven, sometimes eight days or thereabouts. The time I lay ten days was at Hackney at my kinsman's habitation, where the Lord gave me visions of their

breaking up, and of the deadness of Gideon's spirit to the work of the
Lord, showing me that he was laid aside, as to any great matters, the Lord
having finished the greatest business that he would employ him in. And
I singing forth their breaking up, Colonel Bingham,[55] which was one of
them, being present, hearing what I spake as to Gideon, and to the rest of
the representative, he was well pleased (as I was told) to call it a prophecy,
saying that he was glad of that prophecy of their breaking up, for he
thought little good would be done by them. This vision I had the third of
the seventh month, called September, at Hackney, 1653.

Then again, within one month after I had at Mr Barrett's[56] home at
Dowgate, more visions concerning the breaking of the same representative, and many other visions I had concerning the nation.

And then again, about fourteen days before the breaking up of them,
I had clear discoveries of the departure of those from the house whom I
had called the linsey-woolsey party,[57] which the Lord said he would not
have in his tabernacle work. But if those whose hearts were upright sat for
temple work,[58] and for the building of that latter house, which Christ saith
shall be more glorious than that of the former, if they come from among
them, the Lord will make them glorious instruments for himself in those
great concernments that he had spoken forth in his word. And upon it I
saw their coming from them, and I sung the passing bell[59] between them;
singing forth another passing bell to those that are in present power now,
nominating him that was the chairman, Mr Rous,[60] the Lord showing me
that his heart was very hypocritical and that he was not for the work of
the Lord. So that I had many songs and discoveries from the scripture
against him, not hearing the least word, but that he was a very godly man,
as creatures said. But what I had against him, it was from the Lord, which
I spake then in the hearing of many, saying though he and the rest of
them (which are now a council) said, "Let us separate from that factious
party, casting them out with the prayers of Christ's poor flock," reporting
that God thereby should be glorified according to that scripture in the last
chapter of Isaiah [Isaiah 66.5]. But I said, "God will appear to your comfort, and they shall be ashamed." This vision I had at Mr Marsh's house
at Dowgate.

After this I went home to Hackney, and the first week I came home,
not knowing anything of the dissolution which was then drawing near, I
had these visions. First I saw a great tower,[61] and the rooms thereof were
like to the council rooms at Whitehall, which I saw strawed thick with
gunpowder; and at a little distance I saw a white tower, for whiteness and
sparkling glory, I never saw anything to parallel with it; and looking into
it, I beheld many very precious saints, with their eyes fixed toward heav-
en, their countenances shining as the sun. And near to them, between
that white tower and the other tower, were a great many of the colonels

and chief of the army, with their pistols cocked and lighted match in their hands, beating the fire upon the gunpowder, endeavouring to drive it up toward the white tower, but they could not, for the fire would not take. Presently upon this, it was said to me, "Whereas thou seest this high tower whereon the gunpowder is, it is a great many men of the wise and politic, grave and judicious so called, that are drawing up together, and their wisdom, power and policy is that gunpowder that thou seest, and the match and army men, or the chiefest part of the army that shall assent and join with that tower and gunpowder against the white tower, saying it was not to destroy the white tower that they were come forth, but the factious ones that sat therein." Presently this scripture likened them to those of the old world, that said, "Let us build a Babel[62] that may reach to heaven" [Genesis 11.4], and God came down and confounded their language, so he will do by these that were rising up against the white tower, as it is written in the Proverbs, "The name of the Lord is a strong tower" [Proverbs 18.10] wherein those factious ones, as they called them, sat in safety, and shall be preserved all their days. *God humbled pride*

Another vision I had at the same time, of many oaks,[63] with spreading branches full of leaves, very great limbed. I looking to the root, which lay but very little in the ground and looked dry, as if it were crumbled to dust; and above the ground was only a little dry bark, on which limbed and spreading oaks were set; a few shrubs which, being by, were very lovely and green, these great oaks fell suddenly down and covered the other. Presently I saw a very lovely tree for stature and completeness every way not to be paralleled by anything that ever I saw, and before which the great oaks crumbled to dust, and the little shrubs were raised up, growing and thriving exceedingly. Then I desired scripture to this vision; reply was, in the first of Isaiah, it is said, "They shall be confounded in the oaks that they have desired" [Isaiah 1.29]; and as to that lovely tree, it was declared to me to be the Lord Jesus, which I had sometimes seen in the New Jerusalem which is spoken of in the Revelation ult., that that tree was the very same that is there mentioned whose fruit should be very many and beautiful [Revelation 22.2], held forth to the shrubs, which they feeding upon should immediately grow up to a lovely stature; "which," said the Lord to me, "thou here seest, that no sooner doth this tree appear, which represents my Son, but immediately those despised shrubs that the great oaks endeavoured to scatter and hide in their holes, they shall come forth, and all the oaks shall crumble into dust; this is not by might, nor by power, or arms, but brought in through the pourings out of my spirit."

Two nights before the Protector was established,[64] I had a glorious sight of a throne, angels winged flying before the throne, crying, "Holy, holy, holy," [Isaiah 6.2–3] unto the Lord, "the Great One is coming down with terror to the enemies, and glory and deliverance to the sincere, and them that walk uprightly"; hearing of this, I broke forth with much melody, singing also "Hallelujah", praise and honour unto thee, O Lord, will I render unto them that thus cry "holy".

Then another vision followed: a great company of children walking on the earth, a light shining round about them,[65] a glorious person in the midst of them, speaking these words: "These will I honour with my reigning presence in the midst of them; others shall die in the wilderness, which wilderness I will show thee by and by". So that departed.

A third vision followed, wherein I saw great darkness in the earth and a marvellous dust like a thick smoke ascending upward from the earth; and I beheld at a little distance a great company of cattle,[66] some like bulls, and others like oxen, and so lesser, their faces and heads like men, having each of them a horn on either side their heads. For the foremost his countenance was perfectly like unto Oliver Cromwell's; and on a sudden there was a great shout of those that followed him, he being singled out alone, and the foremost; and he looking back, they bowed unto him, and suddenly gave a shout, and leaped up from the earth with a great kind of joy, that he was their supreme. And immediately they prompting him and fawning upon him, he run at me, and as he was near with his horn to my breast, an arm and a hand clasped me round, a voice said, "I will be thy safety." He run at many precious saints that stood in the way of him, that looked boldly in his face; he gave them many pushes, scratching them with his horn, and driving them into several houses; he ran still along, till at length there was a great silence, and suddenly there broke forth in the earth great fury coming from the clouds, and they presently were scattered, and their horns broken, and they tumbled into graves. With that I broke forth, and sang praise, and the Lord said, "Mark that scripture, 'Three horns shall arise, a fourth shall come out different from the former', which shall be more terror to the saints than the others that went before' [Daniel 7.8,20–21]; though like a lamb," as is spoken of in the Revelation [Revelation 13.11], "in appearance a lamb, but pushing like a beast," being not only one, but many and much strength joined together.

Thus far it was conceived meet and requisite to represent the spirit and condition of the party. Not from thence to borrow the more esteem, or belief to the relation following (let that adventure forth upon its own score, and stand or fall in that spirit that gave it being), but that the truth may shine forth, as to the particular state and condition of the party, through that cloud of unchristian condemnings, odious censures, and black defamations of unsatisfied, interested, envious, and unbelieving persons which are gone forth; whereby, that in this dispensation, which to many that were witnesses of it seems to be the glory and beauty of it, may be confounded and darkened, and the eyes of them that would see, be blinded in judgement.

Now concerning her speaking in Whitehall, this account we have to offer of
the state and condition of her spirit in that work, which was received from her
own lips in the hearing of some then present, in answer to the questions which
the relator moved unto her. One question was asked her some weeks after she
left Whitehall, and was this: "What frame of spirit was upon you in uttering
those things in Whitehall? Was it only a spirit of faith that was upon you, or was
it vision wrapping up your outward senses in trances, so that you had not your
senses free to see, nor hear, nor take notice of the people present?" She answered, "I neither saw, nor heard, nor perceived the noise and distractions of the
people, but was as one that heard only the voice of God sounding forth unto
me." Besides her own word, the effects of a spirit caught up in the visions of
God did abundantly appear in the fixedness, and immovableness of her speech in
prayer, but more especially in her songs, notwithstanding the distractions among
the people occasioned by rude spirits, that unawares crept in; which was observed
by many who heard her, who seemed to us to be as one whose ears and eyes
were locked up, that all was to her as a perfect silence.

Another question was, "What moved you to silence at any time when you
ceased from speaking? Was it with you as with other good men, ministers etc.,
who cease at discretion, either having no more to say, or having spent their
strength of body, or having wearied the people?" She answered in these words,
"It was as if the clouds did open and receive me into them; and I was as swallowed up of the glory of the Lord, and could speak no more." To give you the
relator's observation for the further persuading him of the truth of this: he took
notice twice in her ceasing from speaking. Once she ended with prayer, wherein
being sweetly and highly raised in her admirings of the glory that she saw, she uttered these, or like, words: "Oh what brightness! What glory! What sweetness!
What splendour!", which last word she hardly expressed in a full sound, and
said no more. Another time ending with a song, in three or four of the last
words, in the last verse, her voice sunk into her breast, that they could not be
understood, like the words of a man falling asleep.

Now follows the relation of so much of her prayers and songs, as by a very
slow hand could be taken for eight days.

* * * * *

Upon the tenth day of the eleventh month, 1653, the relator, coming into the
chamber where she lay, heard her first making melody with a spiritual song,
which he could not take but in part, and that too with such imperfection, as he
cannot present any account of it to the understanding of others. After her song,
she without intermission uttered forth her spirit in prayer, wherein among many
other, she expressed the passages following:

What is marvellous or can be in the eyes of the Lord? The resurrection of Jesus was marvellous in our eyes [Psalm 118.23], but not with the Lord, for nothing could keep down a Jesus. Thy people could never have come out of their graves, had it not been for the resurrection of Jesus; as thou risest, so should they, as thou diest, so should they, thou wilt make all things death before them. What endeavourings were there to have kept thee in the grave? Oh, but what fastness, what locks, what bolts that could keep in a Jesus? Oh, but they thought that the Lord Jesus was but a man, they understood not that the divine nature was wrapped up in him in the human nature; when thy time came the sepulchre was open,[67] and the Lord Jesus came forth with great power and majesty. Oh blessed be the Lord that brought forth the Son, the heir, him that was victorious over his enemies; so shall there be a declaration against all things that would keep thine down. Faith is that victory; how so? Because faith brings into the bosom, and it draws forth the death and resurrection of Jesus upon us: thou art a-bringing forth a great resurrection.[68] Jesus Christ is upon his appearing; there are some do think so, but they say it is not yet begun, God will bring it about another way, and another time; but the Lord says he will cut short his work in righteousness. Thou knowest who are the Babylonians[69] that are now about thine; as thou didst to thy people of old, thou will come forth speedily, —[70] thy thoughts are so exceeding high and glorious that none is able to reach them; man cannot bring forth his own thoughts; they are so tumultuous, and run unto the ends of the earth; oh then what are thy thoughts O Lord, — though the enemy begin to jeer them concerning those blessed songs. Well, says God, are my people jeered concerning their excellencies, their songs, their hallelujahs that are of my own making, that are before my throne?[71] The Lord cannot endure that these excellencies of his saints should be trampled upon, which are so perfect, so pure. How pleasant are the songs of thine, when they are brought forth out of the churches of thine enemies. — 'Tis not all the force in the world that can strike one stroke against thine, but thou sufferest them to come forth to try thine. Oh that thine could believe thee for thy breakings of them, as well as for thy bindings up; all things under the sun, all things before you, in you, shall work for your good. When they come to understand more of the mystery, and of the entrails of scripture, how will they praise thy Highness? The enemies are strong, Satan is strong, instruments are strong, temptations, they are strong, what strengths are against thy flock! They cannot be without the lion, and lion-like creatures. Oh if thy servants suffer, let them not suffer for passion or rash words, but as lambs. There is a zeal which is but from nature, a man's own spirit may prompt him to, (but the zeal of God is accompanied with meekness, humility, grief for Christ)— Since thy handmaid is taken up to walk with thee, thy handmaid always desired that she might be swift to hear, slow to speak [James 1.19], but now that thou hast taken her up into thy

mount [Exodus 24.12; 2 Peter 1.18], who can keep in the rushing wind
[Acts 2.2]? Who can bind the influences of the heavenly Orion [Job
38.31], who can stop thy spirit? It is good to be in the territories, in the
regions, where thou walkest before thy servant; (oh how glittering, and
how glorious are they, what sparklings are there!)— Thou hast a great gust
to come upon the earth, a great wind that shall shake the trees that now
appear upon the earth, that are full of leaves of profession;[72] but they have
nothing but outward beauty, an outward flourish, but thy trees O Lord,
they are full of sap [Psalms 104.16]. A great number of people said, Oh let
our oaks stand, let them not be cut down. Oh but says the Lord, I will
make you ashamed in the oaks that you have chosen [Isaiah 1.29]; and because you will have these oaks, I will now give you other oaks, and what
are they? A first, a second, and a third power [Daniel 2.36–45], and thou
breakest them one after another. Oh thine own have had a great hand in
these things; thine have said, (We will have oaks and gardens, how have
they run to and fro!) Says the Lord now, I will give you gardens; but they
shall have no springs in them, they shall be as dry chapped ground, they
shall be as the fallow ground. What loveliness is there to walk upon fallow
ground? (You shall have stumbling walkings upon them, you shall have no
green grass in these gardens. What have all the gardens of the earth been?
They have been to thine places of stumbling.) O thou wilt by these thy
strange ways draw up thine into thy upper and nether springs. Thou hast
deceived thy saints once again about these gardens. Let them now run
after them no more, but be ashamed and abashed. We have hankered from
mountain to hill, we have said salvation is in this hill and in that, but let
us say so no longer. When we shall thus be drawn up to thee, then we
shall prosper, and thou wilt give us vineyards, and gardens, and trees of
thine own, which shall abide. — Thou calledst thy servant to come sometimes near this place, to witness against some who said that the kingdom
was already given up to the Father, and contemned the man Christ; but
now hast thou sent thy servant again to witness for thee, for the kingdom
of thy Son.

*Having uttered much more in prayer, which the relator, because of the press
of people in the chamber, could not take, she delivered the further enlargements
of her heart in a song, so much whereof as could be taken, is presented to you
as follows:*

When Babylon within, the great and tall[73]
With tumults shall come down:
Then that which is without shall fall,
And be laid flat on ground.
Oh King Jesus, thou art longed for,

Oh take thy power and reign,
And let thy children see thy face,
Which with them shall remain.
Thy lovely looks will be so bright,
They will make them to sing.
They shall bring offerings unto thee,
And myrrh unto their King.
For they know that thou dost delight
To hear their panting soul;
They do rejoice in thy marrow,
And esteem it more than gold.
Therefore thou hearing their hearts cry
Thou sayst, Oh wait a while!
And suddenly, thou wilt draw near,
The world's glory to spoil.
Oh you shall have great rolls of writ
Concerning Babylon's fall,
And the destruction of the whore,
Which now seems spiritual.
Come write down how that Antichrist,
That is so rigid here,
Shall fall down quite when Christ comes forth,
Who suddenly will appear.
Come write down how those sparkling ones
Which Antichrist are too;
Those notioners, oh do write down,
How he will make them rue.
Come write also that great powers shall
From off their thrones be cast;
Oh the Lord he will batter them,
Though they mount up so fast.
Oh write that the great[74] councillors,
That now 'gainst Christ agree,
How Christ will never own at all,
Nor give them any fee.
Write how that Protectors shall go,
And into graves there lie;
Let pens make known what is said, that
They shall expire and die.
Oh write also that colonels
And captains they shall down.
Be not afraid to pen also,
That Christ will cast them[75] down,

Because they have not honoured God,
They have not paid their vows;
But only blustering oaks have been
Great tall branches, and boughs.
Which have no spirit nor moisture then
How can they longer stand,
Though they a while[76] have active been:
Yet they must out o' th' land.
The Lord will reckon with them all
And set their words before;
They have not brought forth righteousness
Nor relief to the poor.
Which they said they would chiefly aye
But their words do not speak,
But all unto their own nets they
Do stretch themselves and creep.
Pen down how all their gallantry,
Shall crumble into dust;
For the Lord he hath spoken, that
To dust they vanish must.
Come sergeants what will you then do,[77]
When your masters are cast,
What will become then of your pay,[78]
Which you run for so fast?
Oh sergeants some of you I have,
Looked on to be such which
Would not have taken such a place,
Your hands forth for to reach.
Poor sergeants that were honest men
Oh how are you fallen,[79]
Oh how are you now taken with
The vanity of men?
Oh sergeants leave off this your work,
And get some other thing,
Your pay'll be sweet to follow him,
Who is your Lord and King.
Oh bread and water is more sweet,
Than roast meat of this sort,
Oh meat of herbs [Proverbs 15.17] better's for you,
And of better report.
You come and crave pardon of them,
While you dissemble in heart,
Oh call for pardon from a Christ,

When to his bar you come.
And leave those other ways which will
Prove injurious to you;
The Lord doth hate such practices,
And he will out them spew [Revelation 3.16].
Oh keep thy poor saints that they may
Not run away from their Lord,
Oh let them be contented with
The morsels thou dost afford,
Oh that they may not now set hands
To engagements that come,
But rather engage for the Lord,
Who is the only Son.
O mind the saints how engagements
Have become to them a snare,
That others they may not them take,
But up to thee repair.
Let them know 'tis but a short time,
That men shall thus[80] abide,
'Tis but a while that these stormy winds,
Shall bring forth such great tide.
Though winds and waves they boist'rous are,
Yet Christ will them rebuke [Matthew 8.26; Mark 4.39; Luke 8.24],
He will speak to them to abate,
And they'll go at his look.

After she had breathed forth this song with more enlargement than could be noted by the relator, she proceeded in prayer which for the press of people crowding and darkening the chamber could not be taken. She continued that day in prayer and singing four or five hours together, and then was silent.
The next day being the eleventh day of the month, the relator came in and heard her in prayer, wherein she delivered many things, some whereof being of public nature were taken, and are presented in the account following.

Must thy servant that is now upon the throne,[81] must he now die and go out like a candle? Oh that thy servant could mourn day and night for him. Oh that he might be recovered out of that vainglorious council, out of their traps and gins! Oh his soul is in bondage, he will not hear New Jerusalem's sermons if thou convince him not! Oh that he might be laid in thy bosom, that he might not refuse to come among thy people. Oh that he might hearken to a praying people, rather than to a wicked council, rather than to a politic crew about him! Father, that he might, Lord God, come out of those fetters and chains. And then do thou show him his work, and his transgression wherein he hath exceeded [Job 36.9], and open his eyes to receive instruction. He is in chains by reason of that outward glory and pomp that is round about him. Oh he thinks he is taught by thee thus to go and to act! Oh but blessed Lord, let they handmaid entreat thee to persuade him. For thy persuasions are more than the persuasions of all the great doctors and rabbis that are about him! O that they also might consider what they do, they have been preachers of free grace to thy people. Let them not now come forth with the voice of Haman, but with the voice of Mordecai;[82] let them be faithful, and say unto him thou art but a man that doth thus, let them not join with that that thou art breaking in pieces; thou wilt not have thine to sit upon thrones now, till all thine shall sit together upon those twelve thrones [Matthew 19.28; Luke 22.30]. Is it not better that he shall pry into the laws of King Jesus, than of those that are about him? He little thinks that they would bring him into jeopardy. Let him not entertain any upon the account that they are grave, wise, judicious men; but let him look whether godliness be in them. Oh but he will say they are godly too! Oh, but let him look at actions, whether these actions do speak them godly! Oh this is a day of Jacob's trouble; thine looked for refreshment, and behold greater trouble, they looked for a birth, and behold it is yet in travel.[83] Many of thy children are put to a stand, and know not what to do; though he doth repulse them yet let them tell him of his sins, and tell him with humility, and with tears, not as those deluded spirits that go running about the streets, and say, We have such visions and revelations, who come out with their great speeches of vengeance and judgement, and plagues. Oh, but thine that come from thee, thou givest them humility, meekness, bowels,[84] and tears. Pluck out those of the council that are thy children, tell them that thou dost not love linsey-woolsey garments,[85] linen and woollen mixed together [Leviticus 19.19; Deuteronomy 22.11], neither in the thrones, nor in any building or temple, or concernment of thine. It is true authorities and powers are by the commission of the most high. He gave commission to the Assyrian to be a rod to Israel,[86] till he had accomplished his work upon Mount Sion, but here is the difference: that was an enemy whom God would destroy with eternal fire, and perpetual burning; but these come forth as brethren, as thy children, and therefore thine do not know how to bear it from them. Oh it is a grief to the heart that they should smite and grieve thy saints. Besides, the kingdom of the Lord Jesus is at hand, all the monarchies of this world are going down the hill. Now is a time that thine should look off from these things, and lift up their head, for their redemption draws near [Luke 21.28]. Now thou requirest a greater going forth of the spirit; what manner of persons ought ye to be in all holy conversation? We are not to be for ourselves, but for Christ. Now the treasury is open and every one is to cast into it; now all is spread open, for all to come to cast in something. Oh come forth thou great builder in thy glory! Oh what sheddings of blood have there been in order to this work! Let there be days of glory; hear the voice of thine, yea thou dost hear them, though thou wouldest have them to wait, they shall not be a-shamed; they that tarry and rest upon thee, thou wilt come and lead them with thy sweet spices [Exodus 30.34]. Oh that the soldiery might now come forth out of their bravery and say, Shall there be some that shall come up to that glorious building, shall they reign in that day, and shall we that have gone forth for the Lord thus far come short thereof, and be laid aside? Oh help them to entreat thee that thou wouldst not spew them out of thy mouth as lukewarm ones [Revelation 3.16], nor let them not be cast out of thy temple. Now is a measuring time[87] that thou art measuring thy own temple, not the world, but thine own saints, there is a little silence from trumpets and battles, and now is a time of silence. Oh but there is a time of the shooting of bullets, and they will come forth again! Oh that thy temple might not fall to pieces, the stones that are joined to the corner stone, that they may not have the hammer come upon them; no, nor any iron tool come into thy work.

Oh let him be willing to part with such things as may hinder the prosperity of his soul; make him out of love with the wine and feasts below, and bring him in love with thy liquors and flagons from heaven! Oh but their veins are so full of blood before, that they have no room, but do thou cast the overflowing blood, and then what can hinder thy work! Oh but can these dry bones live [Ezekiel 37.3]? Give thy handmaid leave to tell thee that thy children are like dead bones now in the valley.[88] But thine say, Lord, thou canst make them live, thou canst bring nerves and bones, and knit them together again. Let thy servant never be silent, till they be brought out of the valley, out of the slimy pit! Oh do thou fill their pools, thou causest rain to come and fill the pools! O fill all places, all things with water from above, that thine may drink thereof; bring forth that water, that may make them warriors for thee, and not any longer for themselves, and let them know that thy servant doth abundantly tender them! O let all that thy servant hath go for Sion; first, second and last breath. Were it not for thine, thou wouldest send the nations into this nation;[89] thou hast a people in this nation, who have thy name upon them, therefore thou wilt not let out the boars, and the wild beasts against them [Psalms 80.13], for they would spare none. Thou hast a few names that are clothed in white, whom thou dost abundantly delight in, and they delight in thee; they commit their way unto thee, and thou wilt not destroy them though they live in Sodom; thou hast many precious lights in the nation, in this city, or it would be suddenly burnt with fire. Oh how beholding is this tumultuous city to thine inheritance!

Oh, sing for Sion songs my soul,
And magnify that grace,
Which will bring Sion back again,
Into the glorious place.
Oh I will pray while that he doth
Appear here on the earth,
The sparkling glory of those that
Are thy most lovely flock.
I will rejoice while I do breathe,
Because I do believe,
Thou wilt some of the soldiery
Again to thee receive.
O Lord when that thou comest forth,
Scales shall fall off their eyes [Acts 9.18],
And then they will look unto thee,
And still they more shall rise.
When th'hast brought them into thy sweet ways,
And paths of pleasure too,
Where they may recreate their souls,
And behold joys most new.
Oh Lord it is delight to me
To hear thy pleasant voice,
Concerning some of the soldiery
That their pikes up shall toss;
And go forth shall fully against
All foes they have within,
As well as against those without,
And cannons they shall bring.
Their armour shall most lovely look,
In those thou dost appear,
Thou art their Colonel indeed,
Every troop for to cheer.
Oh every regiment of thine
Thou sweetly wilt them speak,
And oh all eyes then shall run[90] down,
They shall eke mourn and weep.
That they have disobeyed the Lord
In bravery so rich,
And in their dainty dishes that
They have with them enriched.
When others would have been glad of
Crumbs that fall from their board,
Many do say still they must have,

Oh these will thine[91] record
Against themselves, and mourn for it,
The Lord will them pass by,
And he will draw them forth again,
And speak them graciously.
O when thou com'st with shamefastness
Oh ye colonels great,
And captains too do ye fall down
Before the mercy seat.
Then he will welcome all of you,
And say, Oh here is that,
Which is more costly food for thee,
And far more delicate
Than all thou hast of that thou stol'st
From the Commonweal poor,
For to feast thy carcass withal,
Which is to be no more.
Oh soldiers shall I tell you of
Great victories indeed!
O come and hearken unto it,
For 'twill supply all need!
You shall no great alarms then,
Nor drums hear from your foes,
You shall not see their spears nor bullets fly
At all you to oppose.
If you will hearken to the Lord,
Which calleth for your hearts,
If you will say, Oh take them, then
You shall not feel foes' darts.
Oh when Christ speaks to you, as well
If soon you do reply,
Not with a flattering speech but with
Sound words to his glory.
Then oh he will give unto you
That which will be much more;
O th'pay that shall come from a Christ
It will throughout thee store.
It will weigh down all flesh surely,
It's heavier than you think,
It is more precious than your ore,
Then do not from it shrink.
Oh soldiers all, that now you were
Upon the mount with me,

That so your songs they may be heard,
When that you come to see.
Oh it will be well worth your time
To follow the sweet lamb
Where'er he goes [Revelation 14.4], oh after him say,
O Lord we come we come [Hebrews 10.7,9].
Oh here is a General, and he
Is a King of them too,
A Protector, Conservator,
Oh draw near him up to.
He'll be all things to soldiery
That their hearts can desire,
Oh he will be weapons to them,
He'll be their match and fire.
Oh he'll be also cannons great,
Grenado pieces[92] too.
Oh muskets he himself brings forth,
To put your hands into.
Oh he will be pikes for you, to
Go after enemies strong;
Oh he will be a sword for you
Against such would you wrong.
Oh he will beat your drums for you,
And your alarms sound,
He will give watchword unto you,
That none shall you confound.
Oh he will also trumpet out
An harmony so sweet,
Which shall make you on geldings mount
And walk upon your feet.
He will be for soldiers that stand
And cleave to Israel,
With the horsemen he will go forth,
And open their wide[93] breach.
It is better to side with him
Which is a King for ever,
Than to the earthly kings below,
Whom pale death soon shall[94] sever.
A soldier he will remain
Till all nations are cast,
And till the remnant[95] doth come in,
Which soon shall draw full fast.
When he calls them then they shall run

And draw near unto him,
He speaks the word, Oh come you forth,
Then do you answer, When?
His voice it is most powerful,
They cannot it gainsay,
But must reply, Oh we come forth
To thee our brightest day.
Oh soldiers do you love always
Him which will go before,
And slay all giants in the world,
And make them roll in their gore.
You have not only to Scotland gone,
But to Holland also,[96]
He sounded forth his voice so high,
And whirlwinds made to blow.
And on the seas oh there he hath
Most gallantly appeared,
When you were struck with sorrows great
He then your heart upbeared.
For then he undertook the stroke,[97]
And smote those foes so high,
Though they did brag and boast, and say
They were great Almighty's.
But oh the mighty which is true
Did their might then confound.
He sunk their ships and slew their men,
Much treasury he drowned.
Oh 'twas the great God on that land
A General was before,
The same Highness did go on sea,
And did appear much more.
A Pilot he went in the ships,
Still did remain and stay,
And turn them about for this land,
Much kindness to convey.
O he it was that drew them on,
And fought for us before,
Oh he it was that broke their masts,
And humbled the great ships all.
Oh he it was that made them run,
And made them hide their head,
It was thy stroke O thou great God,
That laid their bodies dead.

Oh 'twas the Lord himself I'm sure,
That stopped the Holland's ships,
That did maintain our landships[98] when
Those Hollanders be split.
And is not these things for to be
Declared and writ down,
When th' hast on our nation so shone,
And them how hast thou crowned?
With mercy and deliverance,
Which is exceeding great;
The loss of many precious ones,
And splitting of great ships.
Oh but the loss of thy dear ones,
Oh is not that to be
Thought on by you that are great ones,
And of the soldiery.
Oh think! Oh remember these things,
Oh again call them to mind,
That you may fresh have God's goodness
And feel his rushing wind [Acts 2.2].
That so more of you may be wise,
Here in this nation great,
That so you may no longer stretch
Yourselves and lie and sleep.
Our father, wilt thou bring to mind
And fasten it on their hearts,
That they may not to themselves[99] that they
Harden not to thy smarts.
Who have been brought along the work
By thee the Lord of glory,
That they may get up to the Lord,
And to his territory.
O thou dear General also,
I would fain have thee to hear,
The Lord Jesus does speak to thee,
Oh come therefore and hear.
Oh hearken unto Christ and hear,
Let not his sound go forth;
But oh do thou gently receive
What he will thee counsel.
Do not hearken to vain spirits,
Nor to counsellors great
Which wicked are and false ones which

Did drive thee to thy seat.
But hearken to sound words which come
From him that is so rich;
Oh listen what the Lord holds forth,
And what he thee doth teach.
That thou shouldst not assume to thee
Higher power than Christ doth give;
But thou shouldst say unto all saints,
Oh come let us here live.
In honour and great dignity,
Which Christ here doth afford;
Oh let us have one only King,
Always t'write our record.
Oh do not thou aspire, for to
So high a title have,
As King, or Protector; but oh
Unto Christ that do leave.
Oh let him be advanced, and
You he will then up raise;
Oh he will give unto thy soul
Most comfortable days.

Therefore Father teach him, let him know that he may reign as one of thine. Oh is it not a sweet thing to be crowned by thee? And that is sweeter than to be crowned by man. Oh, says Gideon! I will not be your king,[100] the Lord shall reign over you. Oh, it is enough for him to be one of thy kings! Oh let him now deny, and cast it down, and say, Without these dignities and great titles, I will serve the people and commonalty; and then wilt thou say to him, Thou art my Gideon. Let him consider that thine shall rule over all nations; and let him say, Why may not this be the time that it does draw near? Let not him say as they said of old, who put the day far from them, that the vision was for many days, for a time yet afar off. But let them accept of the day and time that thou hast put into their hand. The Lord is building his temple, it is no time now for them to build tabernacles. Now thou art upon thy temple-work, shall they be building great palaces for themselves? The soldiers slight thy handmaid, but she matters not, they shall and must consider in time. They say these are convulsion-fits, and sickness, and diseases that make thy handmaid to be in weakness. But oh they know not the pouring forth of thy spirit, for that makes the body to crumble, and weakens nature. In these extraordinary workings thou intendest to show what is coming forth hereafter; something is a-coming forth, there is so Lord; and oh how does thy handmaid bless thee!

Having prayed for, and made much mention of the merchants, she sings the following hymn to them.

O merchants! oh turn to the Lord!
What he to you reports,
Look into the written word so sure,
And see what he brings forth.
Oh do not grieve at losses great,
Though all your ships do split,
Oh look to that bottom wherein
Cannot come any leak.
O take up now your time for that
Which is precious and most sweet,
And shall be given forth to you,
That will receive meat.
Oh merchants! I fain would that you
Might have true gold indeed;
O I desire sweet preserves, which
Christ unto you doth leave.
The sweet preserves come from the seas
And from those foreign parts,
Which are made up by those Indians
That are so full of arts.
You have your canded[101] ginger, and
Your preserved nutmegs too;
That so you may delight therein,
And your mouths overflow.
But oh, there's canded things indeed,
Which is covered with gold,
There is not such preserves as they
Which shall be turned to mould.
But these preserves continue shall,
No mouldy skins shall be
At all of them; but the longer
You keep them, you shall see
They are as fresh and lovely as
They were when first he brought,
They do not lose their taste at all,
Oh that you would have sought.
These things indeed as pleasant, all
That you would feed upon
Them which will strengthen you always
And lead you to Mount Sion.[102]

Oh merchants clothe yourselves with robes,
Which will never be wore
Not that which will to rags be turned
Nor that which can be tore.
But here is clothing substantial;
Oh it is costly too!
Oh it is white! Oh it is that
Which Christ's blood bought to you [Revelation 7.13–14]!
That you might be clothed herewith,
And herein still may go,
No nail nor splinter can these tear,
Nor can remove the show.
'Tis glorious and substantial too,
And it abides for ever,
No enemy can rent it from,
Oh none can it you sever.
Oh merchants then lift up your heads,
Though losses you may have;
Oh the more of Christ do you now beg,
Which will make you most brave.
O you that are proud, and with stout necks
And mincingly do go,
With your black spots and powdered locks
Thinking to make a show.
And so you go unto those which
Are carnal hearts with you,
But oh the spiritual do see,
They do hate it, and spew.
They cannot endure your company,
Oh cover then your skins,
Remember when that Adam fell,
He covered was leaves in.
His nakedness with leavy skins,
At length must be his clothes;
Oh therefore all you naked ones,
Oh do not scripture oppose.
Oh you that sport it forth with that
Which is jesting most vile,
The Lord himself does to you say,
That he will you rob and spoil.
O you that think to do that which
Is injury to saints;
O the Lord he draws them more unto

His lovely open gates.
Where he takes them into himself,
When others are shut out,
Then Mordecai must be called in,
Haman must hang without.[103]
O thou dear Lord, they chains would do
Thine injury therein,
They cannot, for the Lord their God
He is their only King.
Oh sing! oh soul! that I am fain,[104]
And do lift up my heart,
Unto thy beloved so high,
Which is exceeding great.
Hallelujah unto Jehovah,
I will without fear sing,
Unto him which creatures all brings forth,
Oh! thou art the great King.
That store and plenty art to thine,
Rivers and streams are there,
Oh thou dost so much love unfold,
That does the heart so cheer.
While it sings songs to others, and
At the mentioning
Of the perfumes and costly things,
Which are esteemed dear.
They must esteem, and count them dear
That receive from a Christ;
For it cost his most precious blood,
To bring forth interest.
Into these royalties it was,
A saviour led therein,
Thy going to the grave oh Lord,
And rising up a King.
Oh he was willing for to be
Crowned with a thorny one;
That crowns unto his children might
Be brighter than the sun.
O he was willing to drink gall
And vinegar so sharp [Matthew 27.24],
That so his saints might drink sweet wine
For to revive their heart.
He willing was, that they should with
Their spears that then were sharp,

Run into his own sides, that so
His children might not feel smart.
But that water and blood might come,
For to cleanse, and throw out
All their defilements that came when
Man he was driven out,
Of that old Paradise, before
A Christ a new one brings,
Which shall abide for evermore,
Where thine shall in it sing.
O how greatly then are those saints
Established by thee,
That hast a rest brought forth to them,
Where they shall always be.
O it is much more better, sure
Than Adam's state before;[105]
O here is one that is so strong,
None can it rend nor tore.
O Saints, love Christ, love him dearly,
That hath for you thus shown
Great dignity, and his power,
Which set you on his throne.
O saints rejoice! O take your harps
Down from your willows now [Psalm 137.2];
And play your tunes unto the Lord,
For none shall make you bow.
Great Babylon it shall not mock,
Nor injure your sweet songs,
In the enjoyment of a King,
That cast out hath those throngs.
O you saints that Christ tarry on,
When he hath taught you play,
His melody shall you sound forth,
In the sunshiny day.
Therefore desire, and wrestle too
By faith and prayer, while
The Lord hath brought you forth from all
That endeavour you to spoil.
O fear not! Do not tremble, but
Go on courageously.
Let prayer, let faith, let zeal go out,
And through your tongues let fly.
O prophets all,[106] do you speak out,

With bold courage for him,
For unto you he shall draw near,
And appear even when
That the rotten walls are thrown down,
And the great chaos falls,
A fabric then that you shall have,
That by faith on him calls.
Oh he will not be slack, though men
They shift and put you off,
Yet he will suddenly relieve,
And let his cannons off,
That shall all forts and bulwarks here,
All foes that do upstand,
Shall be laid flat upon the ground,
And thine shall enter the land.
O, Canaan, saints you are gone into
That is the pleasant land,
Where you shall eat his grapes most sweet
And that in his due time.[107]
Oh they are fruit that are most sweet,
They are not rot within,
They have no blemish in them all,
He will fill you to the brim.
You are my Joshuas and are
My Calebs[108] that I love,
And you also do show to me
That you climb up above,
Oh unto you I now do speak
They shall go on apace,
And enter into Canaan's land,[109]
And dwell in those sweet rays.
Therefore take heed oh Israelites,
How do you speak and pray
Unto the feeblest of the flock,
To keep them from the way,
Wherein they shall green things behold
And milk and honey eat,
Oh therefore awaken them not
Do not the sickly beat.
But like true Calebs do go forth
With courage bold and stout,
And speak well of God's Canaan,
Which others seek to rout.

Oh do go tell the goodness of
The place and might therein,
The fortifications thereof
Which are made by our King,
Oh speak well of your Canaan,
And of its bulwarks there,
Oh tell of its most glistering walls,
And tell what can compare [Psalm 48.12–13].
What rooms, what walls, what hangings can
Set forth of what is there?
What meat and drink, can be to that
Which is so sweet and clear?
I tell you God will take it well,
When well you do report,
Concerning his sweet Canaan,
And his salvation cups.

Another Hymn.

Oh blessed Lord, be thy great name
That prisoners shall go free,
Out of the prison-house thou bringst [Isaiah 42.7],
Redemption comes from thee.
Oh those that are thine enemies
And rebels were also,
Thou hast captived captivity [Psalm 68.18],
That forthwith they may go.
Though in that inner prison yet
Thou sayst, Oh come you foes,
For here is redemption spoken,
By Jesus is broke out.
Oh come to him, though you have been
Slaves and vassals to sin,
Yet his Father's free grace he doth
Unto your souls eke bring.
And saith, O rebels I came forth,
That so you might be changed,
And of rebellions made such which
Shall with Christ ever reign.
Oh come, saith Christ, you captives
That Satan hath held under,
Oh if you look upon a Christ,
Your foes shall not you plunder.

That he to's enemies should come
And make them his dear friends,
Calling them not his servants more,
But choice and only friends [John 15.15].
Oh report of your saviour,
That is a prophet too,
And hath treasures provided with
For every moment new.
O speak well of your saviour
Which as a King appears,
Go declare him that is the Lord,
And wipes away your tears [Revelation 7.17].
Oh go forth saints, express your love
To this dear Jesus Christ,
Though some may despite show to him,
Yet open wide your eyes
Unto him, for to you he'll come,
And also shall to others,
That with temptations are scorched,
And are so full of smothers.[110]
Oh that thy saints that are cleansed,
Would to others the oath
Publish of grace and goodness which
In person he breathed forth.
Oh notioners[111] they shall go down,
At the sound of him which
Will not them fail who do him love,
But he will to them reach
His arm for their salvation, and
Puts them in his bosom [Isaiah 40.11],
Though sin and Satan would most fain
Yet they cannot there come.
For thou hast hedged thine about,
And thou hast locked them in,
O none can fetch and drive them forth
From the most mighty King.
Oh the longings of poor souls sure
To see thy countenance!
Oh if the world did him behold,
Oh they would prize his glance.
When creatures are in dungeon dark
They prize one beam of light,
Much more do thine when they do see

Beams of thy lustrous light.
Oh they that have a while been starved
And pined with hunger been,
Oh they will prize any relief
From it they will not fling,
But eat it gladly, and will praise,
And then what may they do,
Whom thou hast brought from chains and from
Satan who would them rue?
Oh Lord then thy spiritual ones,
The more of thee they eat,
The more of thee they do desire,
Thou art so excellent sweet.
Such honey and such wine as which
Does drop from thy sweet spring
Oh they desire to reach forth, and
Most kindly take it in.
Oh they Lord, that have felt the cold,
And in the storm have been,
Oh how they will breathe after thee
And crowd under thy wing!
And thou their Lord wilt cover them,
From all the bitter storms,
They shall be kept under thy wing [Matthew 23.17],
And freed from the world's harms.
Oh it is Lord, oh it is sweet
To draw thee forth at length,
It is thou Lord that must draw out
Thyself, thy height, and breadth.
For when thou hast drawn up to thee
Oh the large field thine is in,
And the many paths where they may walk
Hand in hand with their King,
Who lovingly doth walk and tell
Of things that shall break forth,
And of the New Jerusalem,
Gloriously thou dost afford.
Oh when thou tak'st such from below
To thee that art so high,
Hallelujahs[112] must go forth through
The heavens and the skies.
Hallelujahs when the sentence shall come forth

Of dread against all those
That are against such a lovely God
And do thy name oppose.

> *These were uttered and sung the twelfth day of this eleventh month.*
>
> *Upon the thirteenth day she uttered many precious things in prayer and songs, which the relator could not for the press of people write down.*
>
> *Here follows some short account of some things she uttered the fourteenth day, as the relator could take them in some scattered expressions.*

Let thy servant beg high springs for saints; come in with full springs, in such a time as this, when that the waters are brought so high, that thy poor children are ready to be overwhelmed by them, in their snares and entanglements; they say these waters are very clear and sweet that come from men, but at length they make the soul very muddy. Why is thy hand-maid so long with thee upon the mount,[113] seeing thy sparkling glory, and those reviving springs, but that thy handmaid may plead with thee concerning thy saints, thine inheritance and that her heart may take in the things concerning thy saints. There is now a great deal of provision for a poor man,[114] and yet he will wither and come to nothing; certainly folly will be writ upon his labour, thou wilt not commend it as a piece of wisdom. Thou wilt not give it a badge of honour, thou wilt rather put a blot upon it, thou wilt never write fair concerning it; thou art coming to write fair concerning the palace of the Lord Jesus, and the glory of that kingdom. Oh but they have a veil over their eyes that they cannot see it. Oh, but says God, I have a Jacob, a dew, a lion [Micah 5.7–8],[115] and they shall know it. I have but a few names among you, in whom my name is found, though I have a great many souls. Thou wilt find, Lord, but a few, that have kept themselves undefiled from the world [James 1.27] that are pure religious ones; there are many fleshly, national religious ones, but the poor, fatherless and widow [James 1.27] are the companions of the pure religious ones. They think it scorn if one should tell them they are not religious, they will say you are censorious. Oh but thou wilt tell them that they do not do that which is pure religion, that is so before God; who is such a burning and shining light as John was [John 5.35], who gives forth such a testimony of Jesus as John did? Is it not said that they who faint in adversity, it is an argument that their strength is small? When they are in prosperity then they can speak large and high things of Jesus Christ, but then hold out in time of temptation, that hath a good report with God. God saith, I will judge righteous judgement, I will not judge what you do, when you meet, and speak and pray together, but I will follow you into your secret places, your houses, your callings, your offices,[116] those that breathe after thee Lord, they are searching after their secret sins [Psalm

90.8]; for thou comest into the heart; they cannot prosper that cover their secret sins, there is such a covering of secret sins, that prosperity flies from us, and takes wings and flies away. —

It is not a time now to raise states, and names, and great things, for thou art now pulling down, they will set up their beacons upon their own hills, when thou sayst thou wilt have thy beacon upon thine own hill, and thy standard set up there, oh how do men set up their posts by thy posts? —

When thou dost make bars and iron gates they will endeavour to break open [Psalm 107.16], and beat them down, that the enemy may come in among us; they think if they have armed men about them it is well with them. O, but to have thy armed men which are chariots of fire about them, that were safe indeed; when thou comest with thy hand, what are all these before thee? They are crushed on a sudden. Take away Lord all that sour leaven[117] that is upon the earth, it savours all the meal, that it has a brackish taste; though many of thy children in their affections and judgements may be soured by this leaven, yet thou hast some into whom this sour leaven cannot enter. Take it out of thy children that are in the midst of the earth, and keep thy lump that it may not be infected; many are infected, their language is infected, it was sweet before, but now it is confused [Genesis 11.7], it had an harmony, but now it hath no relish.[118]

Thou hast declared the coming of the Lord Jesus, that he shall come suddenly, so the transactings of things here below do come suddenly, and poor man, how is he confounded, he is in a smother in his own judgement, he is in the smoke, and cannot find the door! Let not thy children be blinded and blood shed, oh take them out and let them take heed that they do not return into such smoky houses again. Oh let thine bless thy name, that thou hast proved a clear flame for their eyes, a burning flame that shall burn up all smoking things, as crackling thorns [Ecclesiastes 7.6] under their feet.

Oh, that thy children should drink up inflaming wine, not like thy inflaming wine, for that's a[119] beautiful inflaming, but an inflaming to redness and burning. —

Thine that thou keepest from such things, they shall walk with thee, thou wilt make them partakers of glorious privileges, thou wilt bring them into thy territories above, into thy sweet walks, how wilt thou hang them about with honeysuckles? Not like the honey that is of the earth, that is clogging, but pure honey that is reviving; thy Ezekiels that behold thee by the river Chebar,[120] oh what sights, what glories, what rivers, what springs do they enjoy and yet thy children are afraid to suffer; oh what a spirit of slavish fear hath seized upon thy own children! Though thou hast said the Lord will be with you in the fires and in the waters [Exodus 13.21–22], yet what pale faces are there amongst thine, oh this is to profess Jesus! —

Thou wilt make the whole earth to be thy children, and wilt make

them to be the honourable ones, and yet they will not know, nor consider
it; oh this is a time not for man to reign, but for the Lord Jesus, and this
voice sounds out here and there by a son or a daughter. Oh, but when
shall all the sons and all the children cry for King Jesus? The reason is, because of the infirmities of the flesh, and because thine are of a stammering
speech, and of stuttering tongue, but thou hast promised that the time
shall come that there shall not be a people of a deeper speech than thy
people, and they shall not be of a stammering tongue [Isaiah 33.19]. Come
oh all you disputants, monarchs, scribes and rabbis of the world, come
forth now, and let us see what arguments you can bring forth against the
spirit, the pourings forth of it, the rising of the Son of righteousness upon
the world, against the influences of the heavenly Orion; oh, you shall be
the men that shall be of a stammering lip, and of a stuttering tongue [Is-
aiah 28.11].[121]

O what a doubting is there now among thine, what disputing, what
reasoning, what they shall do, whether they shall cry up a man or King
Jesus; let them take the engagements of man and lay them under their
feet, and take the engagement of Jesus, and lay that to their heart. Let thy
servants now be of a public spirit, let them now fly high above the skies,
not into vain conceits, vain speculations, and high notions; oh but thou
callest to an exalting high through Jesus unto thee; they that have kept to
a crucified Jesus, they are thine. Oh, here are good words, great allegories,
and high expressions, oh, but they that honour thy Son thou wilt honour
them; they that honour the Son, honour the Father [John 5.23]; oh they
that say they will honour the Father alone, and live in the Father alone,
and lay aside the Son, they are deceived, thou wilt have them keep within
thy bounds, and not to stretch the point beyond the compass. Oh let
thine take a thorough view, and not rashly take up anything. Thou wilt
have thine try the gold as well as the dross [Proverbs 25.4; Ezekiel 22.18;
Zechariah 13.9; Malachi 3.3]; thou wilt not have thine take up anything,
while they know not the life of it.

Oh, but who is he or she that admires the Lord Jesus through all, in all
and above all? He is all in nothing creatures, the creature is nothing, but
thou hast said thou dost great things through nothing. Oh, that thine
were taken with truth for truth's sake, that they would seek into the bottom, and I go into the golden mine, and not only gather up the shavings
thereof, let them not take up the sparks but the fire itself.

That a poor creature should subsist without sustenance, what a gazing
is there at this poor thing, while you forget the glory that is in it, go into
the marrow, what matters it for the bone, let them have the spirits, it is
no matter for anything else, —

Oh that thy poor servant should thus long converse with thee, and so

long sit at thy fire, and feel the warmth thereof, and so bear testimony
against all false fires, and all things that are against King Jesus.

Then she uttered forth this song, the greatest part whereof, as much as the
relator could take, runs as followeth.

Oh, it is that light that burneth bright
A flame that is so clear
The soul and tongue, yea every part
Unto thee shall draw near,
And praiseth his free grace for all,[122]
And sets out Jesus too,
Who came forth from the Father's seat
To bring that love unto,
Which is a fire so hot and which,
Its warmth gives forth most clear;
Oh 'tis a fire that is brought forth
By him that paid full dear.
Oh, when thy love sent out thy Son,
He sweetly did reply,
That he would hasten through the earth,
And on the cross would die.
Oh, when love did warm his bosom
There was no stay at all,
But the Lord Jesus he did reach
Forth that which was royal,
And saith that love had sent him forth
To die for rebels great,
That they might come that enemies were
Unto this mercy seat;[123]
And he did fulfil his great work
With courage that was bold,
That there might come forth unto his
That pure and beaten gold,
Which was for to enrich them that
Before were poor and mean,
Who hath bestowed here on them
A glory pure and bright.
Which none can purchase by their worth
Nor treasure that is here,
For free grace it is to them rich,
And bids them come full near,

Where they may have that which will make
Them rich for ever more,
And will be always unto them,
A bright and golden ore.
Where no dross shall at all it reach,
Nor cover it from sight
To those that Christ doth bring it for,
Who tells them 'tis their right.
And therefore saith, Receive of him
Who purchased hath for thee,
Redemption out of all thy filth
And from thy slavery,
Rather than all crowns and palaces
Wherein you do delight,
Oh covet more the brightness of
Him which doth make us white.
Oh 'twas indeed great love that such
Which are so black below,
Full of the spots of filthiness,
That thou shouldst love them[124] so.
He that was God-man[125] understood
The love was in the Father,
Who none can see nor can show forth,
But he that was his lustre.[126]
O thou most dear and only Lord,
That lookest down below,
Who in thy love thy spirit brings forth,
And it doth on us blow.
Oh it is it which doth maintain
All vitals that are within,
Oh, it repairs all parts throughout,
And filleth to the brim.

Then raising her note she proceeds as follows.

O King Jesus,[127] King Jesus, thou
In apparel art rich,
A diadem about thy neck,
And forth it thou dost reach.
Of thy rich diadems to thine,
And of thy crowns of pearl,
And thou sayst unto thy poor flock,

Oh I will make you earls.
Oh, I will make you potentates,
And then believe my word;
For it is true, says Jesus Christ,
Look into my record,
And see whether I have not declared
What you are unto me;
Also what I am for your sakes,
And that you shall me see;
And look into the written[128] word,
And there you shall behold
How I have beautified and have
Made you as bright as gold.
O look into the written word,
And there drink you of me [John 6.54–56],
For I am flagons of wine and,
You shall partake of me.
Oh sit down at my table [Luke 22.30], says
The Lord who is so high,
And I will come and fill you, and
I'll open wide your eyes,
That you shall me behold therein,
In all my counsels here;
You shall see how I am the chief,
And your most choicest dear.
O look into the written word,
And see the blessings there
To servants that do wait for him,
That is so high and dear.
He says he will come forth to them,
And gird himself about [John 13.4],
And set him down on them about,
Where none shall cast them out;
O when that Christ he forth doth come,
As a servant he doth speak,
That he will wait upon them [John 13.4–15],
While they eat upon his meat;
He'll fill their cups and flagons too,
He will say, Drink O friends,
O drink, O drink abundantly [Song of Songs 5.1].
For oh, I will you spend.
Oh draw near,[129] says Jesus Christ,

And come and now reply,
And say unto the living Lord[130]
That up on high you'll fly.
You are my rare ones and you are
The darlings that I love,
Oh come, oh come, says Christ the Lord,
Go up with me above.
Come hither, come hither, says Jesus to
The regions that are high,
Oh draw up to the mount of God
To Jesus Christ on high.

And you shall see devouring fire [Isaiah 29.6, 30.30]
Upon your enemies,
But I will be a light to you
And up[131] you shall straight rise.

O you shall rise indeed you shall,
When others they shall down,
Then you shall be raised up with me
When I myself shall crown.

Did they believe what in thy word,
Reported is and penned down,
They would not then to men forth run
And cry them up and crown.

Oh if they did believe the Lord,
What he doth them declare
Concerning the coming of Christ,
Oh then they would him fear.

Oh if they did believe thee Lord,
What thou dost say to them,
Concerning that true holiness
Which shall appear as then.

When thou com'st out then holiness
Abundantly shall flow,
Sincerity and righteousness,
Oh then they[132] shall up go.
But now here's great transgression

In men, they are corrupt,
Oh they are taken with fleshpots,
And with their sinful cup.

Oh blessed Lord do thou draw near,
Do thou speak to them that
Which may now raise them up again
And may lay all flesh flat.

*Having uttered forth this song (as she did all the rest) with melodious voice,
she proceeded to prayer without any intermission, some things wherein were as
follows.*

It is not now as it was in times past, that a kingly progeny should
reign, for that was but for a time, and after[133] they should be judged, destroyed, and taken off, and be no more, and then should the kingdom of
the Lord Jesus come forth, and all the kingdoms of man thrown down before it; and how has thy servant disputed, declared, remonstrated and appeared in the field against Antichrist, and how is his language now confounded? It was the language of Canaan, but now it is the language of
Ashdod.[134] —

Oh thy servant (*speaking of herself*) must now come forth against the
great rabbis of the world. Oh thou knowest that thy servant hath often
wrestled with thee, that thou wouldst employ some other, but thou hast
overruled her, and hast put her to silence; and shall I not be willing to do
or suffer thy will?

And thou givest strength unto her, and bearest up the spirit of thy servant to go through with the work, thy servant is not an enemy to these
men, thou knowest, but a friend. Oh it is for thy sake, and for thy servants' sakes, that thy servant is made a voice, a sound, it is a voice within
a voice, another's voice, even thy voice through her. Thy servant knew
that she was beloved of thee, and that she lay in thy bosom from a child,
and there she might have lived without the condemnings or reproaches of
men, or of this generation; but since Father thou wilt have it so, thy will
be done. If the body suffer never so much, if it be for thyself, thy saints,
thy kingdom, it is better for her than to be in her own habitation, and in
pleasant gardens; and when thy servant has done thy work, she shall be
willing to lock up herself in her closet again, and not to be seen of men.
Oh Lord thy servant knows there is no self in this thing.

*Having further in prayer made mention of the university-learning and the na-
tional clergy[135] (as they are called) she proceeded unto singing, seven or eight of*

*the first verses of the song could not be taken by the relator, it being evening,
and no light in the chamber; the rest were as follows.*

For human arts and sciences,
Because you dote on them
Therefore the Lord will others teach
Whom you count but laymen,
For you have set too high a price
Upon your learning here,
Oh that makes Christ for to come out,
And from you it to tear,
Because you have the honour received,
So much fleece from Christ's flock,
Therefore now you shall be by Christ
Oh made a stumbling block.
Christ's scholars they are perfected
With learning from above,
To them he gives capacity
To know his depths of love.
Oh you because y'have not kept in
Within your bound and sphere,
Therefore the Lord hath declared
He'll put you in great fear.
Though learning it be very good,
When in its place it stands,
But when it gaddeth forth thereout,
It looseth its great bands.
For in the chimney the fire is
Useful and precious,
But when the rafters it doth reach,
It sets on fire the house.
And so is learning when you keep
It within its true bound,
But when you join it unto Christ
He will it then[136] confound.
Oh you have been so gallant, and
You have in silken walked,
O you in dainty food have been,
That hath made you to talk;
But when that they cease putting in
To your wide mouths that gape,
O then you'll cease speaking that, which
Before you did relate

Concerning the sweetness of Christ,
Your studies had drawn out,
O Christ I'm sure he will you try,
Whether you truly spoke out.
For your trial will be when that
Your revenues shall go,
Then it shall be made manifest
Whither your wind shall blow;
But I well know that those that are
True prophets of the Lord
Will live upon that pay which he
Declared in his word [Luke 10.7; 1 Timothy 5.18];
And if they'll trust and venture him,
Oh he will then provide,
They shall not want nor be athirst
That swim within Christ's tide.
Oh is it not better to have
Your pay from Jesus Christ,
Than from those which do roam into
The poor his interest.
The Lord Christ doth against them speak,
They shall not long endure,
The Lord will set his fire to them,
And it shall them devour,
And shall upon them fly about,
And unto ashes go,
And by the floods it shall be washed,
Floods shall it overflow.
Oh do not then, oh rest not in
Your greatness you have here,
For everyone that's high will Christ
He'll put into great fear.

She proceeded again unto prayer, and among many other, expressed these following passages.

They that are thy true seers[137] shall stand, when they that are false seers shall fall and wither and die; the true seers they shall go on and prosper, thou wilt provide for them sufficient maintenance.[138] Oh, let not men think that thine do cry down the ministry of them that are full of the ministerial office, and of thy spirit, and do speak from thee. But there are that are called ministers, that do deny Jesus Christ his coming to set up his kingdom, oh thine would have them thrown down before thee, the Lord will not let there be a famishing of the Word in the land; and he will take care of them. Let there not be a cry among them, that if maintenance go down, the ministry will down; let them know that thy servants are not enemies to them that are truly taught of thy spirit. Let them look into the scripture, and there see what is the true ministry, and what is their pay. Let them see what those were who were thy true ministers, were they such as did pamper their bellies, and their backs? Were not thine willing to feed upon anything, to go in skins, to be anything for the gospel of Jesus Christ? Has not their fulness brought blindness upon them? Oh, where has been that marrow and fatness flowing forth from them? Oh, let there be more of that, thou wilt delight in such as delight in thee, they that delight to serve table more than thee, and thy flock, thou wilt not serve them, whatever judgement or opinion they are of. — Is not the narrative come from heaven concerning what thou art a-doing? Oh, let all thine know it in time; they that are such, as are true students, do thou fill them more and more, let them come forth as trumpeters with a full sound, for if they give forth an imperfect sound [1 Corinthians 14.8], how shall the horse prepare to the battle?[139] Let them not go forth with the sound of their own minds, and their own carnal studies;[140] but with the sound of thy spirit, and that is a right sound, and such will follow thee with timbrels,[141] and with music. O let such rejoice evermore, and let them pray continually [1 Thessalonians 5.17]; oh, they love always to be praying, they can never be weary; not that prayer that is called a gift, or an habit, but it is a spirit, it is the outgoings of thy spirit, it is an harmony that they that have only a gift cannot understand, and it is but like a beating of brass [1 Corinthians 13.1]. True prayer is an excellent talking to the most high, it kindles up the affections, and soaks into the judgement; for thy people are accounted by the world a people of much affections, but of little judgement;[142] but by this thou dost try thy people, for they that have little affections do soon change their note; but they that have sound judgements, soaking judgements, and then the affections right set, they centre then in thee alone, every way the soul is raised that is indeed wrapped up in thee; there are raptures in the tongue, and in the brain, but the raptures of the heart no floods can drown, no fire can quench [Song of Songs 8.7]; the tongue, and the fancy, and the natural life may be taken away, but the spiritual sense, that returns into the sun.[143] Oh what is the carcass, the vessel? They are nothing, but when these are gone, then where am I, but there where I am made perfect in thy self; thou wilt bring thine into the grave before thou raisest them up to live, till thou comest and puttest a sentence of death upon all things here below, they will not look upon that which is glorious.

Here she passed off from prayer to singing; some, or most, of the song was taken, and was as follows.

O that they may say unto death,
O death, where is thy sting,
O grave, where is thy victory [1 Corinthians 15.55]?
Over them thine shall sing.
When they do through death up-mount
Unto eternal life,
O then their hearts and speeches too
Shall run to thee most rife.
O till they see grim death before,
And its most ghastly looks,
They would not mount up unto thee,
To see thy pleasant looks.
Till they do feel his biting teeth,
Their tongues will not sing to thee,
O therefore let them it behold,
Pale-faced death[144] let them see.
They will then pray to thy rich grace,
Thereto they then will fly,
They will to the most high then mount,
And that with open eye.
They shall look on the sun so bright,
And on its beams of grace,
Which doth appear, and cometh forth,
And on them casts its rays.

The four last words of the last verse are added by the relator, who could not take the maid's own words, her voice as it were dying, and sinking into her breast, with which she closed for that time.

The fifteenth day, being the first day of the week, she began with prayer, the principal things whereof are noted in the following account, in the language they were delivered by her, though much more largely than the relator did, or could, take them from her.

He that is entered into rest [Hebrews 4.1–11][145] hath ceased from his own works, as God did from his. Where Lord dost thou take up thy rest? O Lord, dost thou take up thy rest in man? Thou art the centre of rest, yet the outgoings of thy rest were upon man; man must have thy breath[146] breathed into him, other created pieces[147] must have thy name, but he must have thy breath. O how great is his fall, and thou hast shown kindness to him; yet he doth not consider, he doth not take notice what he fell from, and what thou hast restored to him. Oh, thy servant loves to travel with thee in these created pieces, to see thee the Alpha and Omega, the great beginning, and the end [Revelation 1.8; 21.6; 22.13]. O

what sights of the world, what fashioning of curious wits can compare with
that infinite wisdom! O that thy breath should be life to man, that thou
shouldest come and breathe upon him [Genesis 2.7], that thou shouldest
give forth substance about a poor shadow, and take counsel about a poor
shadow. Oh Father, what disputes there are about the soul's mortality and
immortality? Oh, it is because they do not thoroughly search into things,
they do see no more than the breath. Oh, who can set it out, who can
give a definition of man's soul, which is the breath of God? Thou Lord
alone knowest what it is! Thine that have conversed with thee in it, do
see it is a most excellent outgoing of God into a poor carcass. It is a most
excellent breath of God into a poor creature. Man's life as considered as
the breath of God, and the work of the counsel of God, oh how watchful
should they be over their breath, that they do not breathe against their
eternal breath, against the work and language of God. When thou hadst
made man, then thou saidst thou hadst finished thy work, and wouldst
take thy rest. Who was this rest? Why, Jesus was this rest from the beginning; he was the prepared rest from the creation. Thou broughtest forth a
seventh day, wherein thou saidst thou restedst [Genesis 2.3; Exodus 20.11,
34.21], and a work wherein thou restedst, and all to show that Jesus Christ
is the true rest, who is the true sabbath day, the prepared rest, the eternal
rest. Oh, that there might be no more wallowing in Satan's fires and quagmires! Oh they do miss of their rest; they do not enter into their true sabbath; they do not see their first day.[148] Let them see Jesus Christ to be the
true rest, the true first day. Thou first appeared as the first day to poor
contemptible creatures, to poor women.[149] Oh Mary, I am thy rest, and
she answered, "Rabboni".[150] When thou appearest to be rest, then how do
they take thee into their bosom, then they see no peace under the sun but
in thee? If he be gone, rest is gone, sabbath is gone, peace is gone; that
bright day of the resurrection, which is brighter than the rising of the sun,
does not then appear. When a poor soul knows not what to do, temptation weighs them down, corruption sinks them; they know not what way
to turn from briars and thorns. Oh, then, thou appears and gives rest, and
makes them go forth with joy and leads them forth with peace, and then
thou makes all melody before them. Tempted souls can tell what it is to
enjoy their maker, they can say he is their only rest. Oh who would not
make thee their rest?

Thou singledst out a day, because thou knewest man's cruelty, and cov-
etousness, that he would not give rest to man or beast; but what is a day,
if thou in a day wert not the rest? The time will come that the whole creation shall have a rest and redemption which shall abide, not for a day, but
shall continue.

Lord it is a fasting day, indeed when thou art a rest, when thou comest
out with a sparkling rest; if thou hadst given a rest in thy ordinary way,

that had been very sweet, oh but a rest in the mount with thyself, a trans-figuring rest among angels with the brightest sun [Matthew 17.2], oh can there be eclipses upon this sun, the sun of righteousness? Who is the same, and there is no alteration, no cloud can cover it.

Who can mix water and oil together? Will not the oil be always above? So thou dear Jesus wilt still be above upon the top; if trouble come, thou sayst be gone. Surely Lord, I will make mention of thy rest for ever [Psalm 132.14]; thy rest hath so many companions with it, peace, and quietness, and regulation throughout the whole man, all is put to silence before it.

Thy servant wondered at those words, The Lord is risen [Luke 24.34], let all the earth keep silence [Habakkuk 2.20]. What, art thou a-coming forth? Art thou putting a stop to all the nations of the earth, their designs and projects, all enemies both by sea and land?

But I will put to silence (saith the Lord) all enemies within. O arise against all inward enemies, and let them be put to silence. Let there be no more the voice of the earth heard in thine; thou hast put the earth in thy poor servant to silence, thou hast made thy heavens to come down into her earth.[151] —

Whom the Son makes free, they are free indeed. Oh freedom indeed, other freedom what is it? A poor freedom; but this freedom within is through the resurrection of thee rising in the soul: there is such an harmonious company, there is such an abundance of thine, when thou puttest the earth to silence. Oh put the earth to silence, that so they may come to the glorious stature of the Lord Jesus, which none can fathom nor reach the depth thereof. —

Oh that poor creatures might not hear of a Jehovah of righteousness, but that they might also receive thee: thou sentest down a ladder to the earth,[152] the human nature of Christ, to gather up our nature to the divine.[153] Oh how did that human nature appear at the bottom of the ladder upon the earth? Oh what steps did he tread, what steps in the divine nature to gather up human nature into it? Thy poor shall lead up to the top, you are kept by the mighty power of God unto salvation.

Oh it is good to walk up that ladder, where there is such precious air, and such sparkling stars, where there is not only seven days' light, but seven thousand, such as none can number. Oh how can any get near unto thee, if they will throw away the ladder? Poor hearts, they marvellously mistake, you cannot come to the Father but by the Son [John 14.6], you must take both together, therefore this rest came forth, that so there might be a completeness, that there might be nothing wanting; every way what a perfect rest is the Lord Jesus? O dear Christ, dear Christ, can any that have taken thee in, hear thee vilified? Couldst not thou keep silence concerning them, and can they endure to hear thee contemned, to hear thee to be called only a form, and to call themselves a Christ? How can they choose but say we will have a scripture Christ? O dear rest, the declaration of thee is marvellous sweet, the declaration tells of thee that thou art the true rest in the power thereof.

Here she seemed to have overflowings of joy and delight in spirit, and poured out her heart in a song, as follows.

Oh thou art rest, eternal rest[154]
    unto thy children dear,
Yea through the great creation
    thou bringst thy rest them near.
Thou wouldst have all things have a rest
    that in the earth do breathe,
Yea also a rest unto fishes,
    thou dost to them bequeath.
O see and learn of plants and trees,
    of gardens and the fields.
A rest there's from the mighty Lord,
    which he unto them yields.
The creatures they have rest, much more
    such that have sense and breath,
Their rest is higher than the other,
    'cause they are th' commonwealth;
That they might be maintained for
    the sons of men herein,
Therefore a rest thou dost provide
    and quietness thou bringst in;
Calling the earth and all therein
    to be in silence, and
To stay from gathering up the field
    to accommodate the land.
O, what an increase through a rest
    there is in the wide sea,
An increase is in everything,
    brought forth out of the clay:
O land, thou dost through rest come forth
    with great increase unto,
Of strength, and otherways from such
    that thou bringst men unto:
What are the birds and cattle there,
    whereon man is fed?
Thou art a rest to weary man,
    who forth and in is led.

O shall all things that here do crawl,
    and beasts that hang their head,
Be more in praises to the Lord,
    than those whom Christ is head.
For they after their kinds do praise,
    much more then shall ensue,
When that the Lord makes kindness come
    through all, he will renew.
Love he doth multiply indeed,
    upon the sons of men,
That he might screw them to the top
    of his glory in heaven.
That they may[155] not like muckworms be
    and like such creatures which
Have no sense for to reach to him,
    which is their King and Liege.
O he is a rest that requires
    all his to draw him near,
And they shall have full sights of things
    which in creation are;
For he will show that sabbath, and
    first day he will bring out
Unto his saints, and he only
    shall draw the quintessence out
Of all things they shall draw the sap,
    that runneth from the root,
And get up into the high tree,
    where none shall go and pluck.
No, none shall be above to see
    thine, when th'are in thy nest;
For they are closed in so round,
    they lodge within that breast,
That none can scar, nor them afflict,
    no musket shot can come;
There is not any can draw their spears
    or at all shoot their cannon.
Though nests in trees may shaken be
    yet thine shall ere remain;
They rest and nest in Jesus Christ,
    his hand shall them sustain.

Here closing her song, she proceeded without any pause to prayer, therein uttering here and there, as the relator could take them, the things following.

The poor carcass shall moulder before thy being, through a sight of thy
bosom thine are dazzled; in thy nest they see none of their own feathers,
but a new nest of thy own making. The very victuals die before thee, that
eternal life that is sweeter than natural life, than all strength, all natural
parts, what are these to it? Father, when thou withdrawest thy glory from
thy handmaid, thou shalt leave so much heat as shall refresh the body,
and her health shall return again from thee to her, thou wilt give her
strength to persevere to the end. Oh when shall men speak forth from the
demonstration of thy spirit? When shall they go forth in thy garments, not
their garments, not with their surplices and tippets.[156] Oh no, they say,
these they have abhorred and put off. Oh but they speak their university
language, their headpiece language,[157] their own sense. Oh but where is
the voice of the New Covenant teaching,[158] are not they hid and concealed? The beast[159] hath got in his foot, and hath mudded the waters;
men are mudded, they speak a little of the New Covenant, a little of thee,
and a great deal of themselves; but thine have hope in thee, they have
confidence that way shall be made that shall be brought to light, which is
thine indeed, men shall not always be content with the outward relation
of the word, without the whisperings of thy spirit.[160] Oh saith Christ,
when I come forth with my power, and spirit, and majesty, then there
shall be more converted; now they think they have done a great matter,
if they have spoken twice a day; oh but have they had spiritual appetites?
Is there quickness in them? Is the Lord Jesus more drawn and set forth by
them? Let them wait that the Lord will come forth more than he did upon
the primitive saints that there were longing and panting after thy coming.

*Here she closed for that day. Upon the sixteenth day the relator came in and
found her in prayer, wherein she uttered, among other things, these which follow,
the chamber being, as at other times, full of hearers.*

If he were not (*speaking of the Lord Cromwell*) backslidden, he would be
ashamed of his great pomp, and revenue, whiles the poor are ready to
starve, and art thou providing great palaces?[161] Oh this was not Gideon of
old,[162] oh why dost thou come to rear up the pillars, the stones which are
laid aside? Tell him, Lord, thou art come down to have a controversy with
him; oh sin will lay thee flat to the earth; oh sin will bring down a dark
smoke into thy judgement, oh sin will hinder that judgement thou
intendest to bring forth in the earth; oh Gideon, is it thy statesmen shall
carry on the work of the Lord, when they are together in brainwork? What
is an headpiece to an heartpiece? O dost thou think to join hand in hand
with headpieces? Oh thou thinkest (because I cry out for heartpieces for
thee), thou thinkest hardly and jealously of me. Oh but thou art deceived,
I am for the Lord Jesus alone, it is neither advantage nor disadvantage to

me, who is set up, or who is thrown down here below, for thy servant, O Lord, is for that pure interest of Jesus. Who would care a rush or a straw, for the interest of man? What are they that are of his chief council?[163] They are the chief men in the places of judicature, but, saith the Lord, I have said that the righteous, who are choice, who are dead to all outward things, they shall be my judges. But they will say, oh but they are godly too; but, saith the Lord, they are such godly as I will have none of, for they are ready to join with any corrupt party that comes forth, they will own anything, and say unto any, You are my king, so they may have their fat, and fleeces [Deuteronomy 18.4],[164] and all bow down to them. Oh but know, the Lord is the great redeemer in Israel, and he is risen now, and will break all yokes [Isaiah 58.6] as fast as they can put them on.

Because the pastors of churches some of them do own thee,[165] will the Lord therefore own thee? Oh no, the Lord will own such only who are true in heart, and in his sight; some of these have made as great an alarm as others, and have appeared as much as others; but now if they must suffer a little, they will fly; oh, this is a base frame of spirit, says Christ, where is a spirit for me? Thou art going up and down the earth to seek where is a spirit for thee that will cast down the Jezebels,[166] there are but a few such, but they are beautiful ones. Oh, thy servant hardly knows a volunteer that will go forth, though they be slashed in the first going on; but thou knowest where such are, oh fetch them out of their cottages and holes where they lie in obscurity; they have kept their garments clean. — Israel would have a king; if you will have a king, saith God, you shall have him in my wrath. So it is now, people are of such a mad frame of spirit, when the Lord says, Do not do thus, they say they will do so, like old Israel, who were murmuring upon every occasion [Exodus 16.7,8; Numbers 14.2,27,29; 17.5; Deuteronomy 1.27]. Because thou hast declared concerning the coming of the Lord Jesus, and wilt give them judges as at the first, therefore because thou dost not give them presently, therefore they will not stay, but will have their own first; when the resurrection did appear, presently the very disciples were doubting and begun to scruple [Matthew 14.31; 28.17]; so it is now, thine have hardly faith to believe the second coming of the Lord Jesus. Oh, say they, We thought it had been by this time, but now we see it is not yet, but for a longer time. — Lord, let it be sounded in their ears, and let them mark it, there will be as great superfluity, as great lust and filthiness, as great wickedness and enmity, yea and greater, than were before; oh they are all for themselves and Satan; doth not he appear in their feasts, in their garments, in their locks,[167] yea, O Gideon, when in thy own family there shall be that shall go naked and wanton? Oh this is found in thy family! David had not such in his family as thou hast, so many of these; and must thou rule a whole nation, and canst not rule thy own family? Oh, thou sayst, I cannot rule them! Canst thou not? saith God, but I will make thee know what I did, to Eli of old,[168] because of his sons. — How can any go and cry out for King Jesus, if they have him not in their own bosom? Oh, he is a sealed one;[169] and they that are sealed ones can go forth for him! Oh Gideon, art thou one of those sealed ones? Then how beautiful would thy walks be? O, but he hath taken away thy glory here from among thy people? Oh Lord, help him to search into his own family; let him consider to have such evil doings, and actings in his own house, and shall he be afraid to reprove in his own family? Oh, then, where is his courage? Will he blind his eyes, and balk as to them? Then he will blind his eyes as to other things; if the Lord Christ do not reign in his soul, he cannot reign for Christ; therefore you doubting Christians, have a care that you have courage given into your hearts from the Lord, and that the throne of Christ be set up there, before you go out to plead against the throne of Antichrist, and the devil and wickedness. — Thou wilt not have thy Son so despised, therefore come you mockers, your bands[170] shall be made strong, you that mock at the goings forth of the spirit of the Lord, at the wisdom that comes forth through fools; I tell you, O ye mockers, your bands shall be made strong, the bands of filthiness, flesh and carnality made strong upon you. Oh is it not better to have the bands of man, than to have the Lord put bands upon you? Can you break the bands of the Lord from off you? O you that have given your strength to the Delilahs[171] of the earth, everything shall overcome you, every thread shall bind you, everything shall close your mouths, you shall be as weak as water, but they that have kept their garments clean, they shall have strength, and might, and they shall stand up for the Lord, and shall have liberty. Oh but you will say, you were free men, and we were in bondage. Oh but if so, where are then the works of zeal? Of love and courage? The works of Abraham? Abraham was for five righteous ones;[172] oh he breathed after such as had deeds, not words of righteousness, oh to be wrapped up in that glorious royalty, to have that complete garment, oh the effects of that are precious, quietness and assurance for ever. — Come, acquaint yourselves with Jehovah. You great professors, and army men, have you not acquaintance with God? Then all you have is nothing; oh do justice, and do it for justice' sake; and thou, Gideon, that hast assumed the highest place to thyself, thou art not only to do justice thyself, but thou art to see justice done in all places, committees and judicatures abroad, that they may not feed upon the poor; thou art not to wallow in pleasures at home, but thou art to be labouring for the Lord; are these like to be thy judges that take any into office whomsoever? Thou art to go forth, thou council (as thou art called), go and see that the flock of Christ have justice done them, oh look to the whole Israel, to the earth, to the whole earth, for the earth is theirs, and so manifest that you love justice and mercy, as you would seem to do; oh remember Absalom,[173] who was of a very fair carriage, and of good words, take him to thee, for thou shalt not have David; Absalom, he was of a lovely nature, that he might steal away the people from his father David, oh do not thou bring in that rubbish now, that thou hast cast out before; they have cried down the king, the court, and such things, and how are your tongues now tipped with their language, if your hearts had not now turned you aside? Oh Gideon, in Scotland[174] thou didst read what great things were going forth against Jacob,[175] and thou wast afraid that thou wast that Jacob, but in the latter end thou didst take in that Jacob was to overcome, to be a conqueror. Why, the Lord saith, if thou be the true Jacob, thou wilt do then as he did, act, and glorify and sanctify the Lord. He was not for great revenues, great increase, though the Lord gave him great increase; if the Lord gave in to your increase it were well, oh but you take it in from the poor, and from God's Israel; oh that you would take up Jacob's practice, as well as you are willing to take in his comforts when you were in the fields.

Having added many other things, she uttered forth a large song, some part and parcels whereof, the relator, as he could understand her words, did take, and they are as follow.

Oh you that are God's diadems,
Wherewith you here do shine,
O you shall sparkle through the world,
In his most glorious clime.
Oh Gideon, would that I could sing
A triumph here for thee,
Oh would I could behold thy work,
To be glorious indeed.
O that I could thee trembling see
Before the truth indeed.
Oh that thy mouth most willingly,
On righteousness would feed.
Oh that thou wouldst drink draughts of that
Which is pure wine also;
That thou wouldst of the truth so pure
Drink, and thereby might'st grow:
O that thou wouldst be like to him
That was the Ninevites' king,[176]
For to confess thy sin to God,
And to abhor thy sin.
Oh do not rage; do not thou fume!
When th'art plainly dealt with,
But rather embrace them than all those

That brave it in their silk,
And tell thee that thou shalt do well;
They do but flatteries speak,
For be sure the Lord hath said that he
Will spoil thy gallantry.
Oh he will cut it off from thee,
Therefore do thou come up,
And beg of him that he should take,
And with his hand thee pluck
Thee from that which displeaseth him
That forth it thou mayst go,
And walk in those regions where thou
Mayst not feel heavy blows.
Oh desire rather a dish of herbs,
Than this thy stalled ox [Proverbs 15.17],[177]
With those rather desire t' sit down,
That strength may be in thy locks;[178]
That no Delilahs so great and strange
With speeches fair and sweet,
May take thee from that which is true,
And exceeding complete.
O wouldst thou have a chair of state,
And have love from a God,
Oh then cleave unto that which is
Recorded in his word.
Let him not imitate those kings,
Which knew nothing of God,
They did not regard what they saw
Or read within thy word,
But he hath a great tone thereof,
He hath his tongue there tipped,
Oh he hath many scriptures which
Come thorough[179] those his lips.
Oh let not him do as those,
But other things him show
What doth belong unto one that
Hath overcome his foes.
It is not his great chair of state,
That shall secure from thee;
When thou, Lord, pluckest him from thence
They sayst it shall not be.
Oh, the Lord then will say to him,
He must not have such food,

Which Queen-mother, as they did call,
Did drink up as a flood,[180]
That swallowed up all in the pulp,
Shall he such juice here take?
Or shall he have such jellies as
Those, whom thou didst forsake?
And take him Lord, and show him it;
Now that he thus begins,
Acquaint him that those flowings will
Increase his flame of sin;
Oh, make him like to wise Agar,[181]
Not too much for to crave,
Lest that he be drawn from the Lord
And his glory deprave.
Poor Gideon, I did pray for thee,
When like Jacob so clean,
Thou hast been valiant in the field,
And there thy foes hast slain.
Oh then! the flock of God loved thee
More than their earthly lives,
They could have given their all for thee
That in the world did rise.
Their privileges here below,
Yea, all, they said, oh take!
So thou wilt keep thy Gideon then,
And him wilt not forsake;
Yea Lord thou knowst thy servant did,
Lord, let her life go for
The life of that dear one abroad,
Who is a man of war.
Thy servant said, Lord, that she would
Lay aside her interest,
And plead for him on his sick-bed,[182]
That he might see the breast,
Where he should be restored to life,
And walk again on earth,
And manage the affairs for thine.
Thy servant said, Lord, pluck,
Pluck him out of the cannon mouth,
And out from the sharp spear,
Oh, take him from all musket shot,
Oh, is not he thy dear?
Thy servant said further to thee,

Oh, raise him from the grave,
And take away his fever strong
Which makes his body rave.
Thy servant said, Oh Lord give him
Cordials from thy dear self,
That he may come and drink of thee
Who art his saving health.
Thy servant little thought, oh Lord,
When to Worcester he did come,[183]
Where he did vows and promises make
For the most blessed Son;
And for the flock of Jesus Christ,
He would soon here draw forth;
But when he came, he did forget
His promise and his oath.
Oh that he should see such a rout,
At Worcester that last war,
And should not mind what he did see
From thee who art so rare;
And when from thence that he did come
Thy flock about his heels,
And they reach out their wedge of gold,
And brought their —
Then into the city he must come[184]
Among the great ones there,
And their great royalties of food
Which, Lord, thou'lt from him tear.
Oh this food and these dainty things,
These pleasures him did smother;
Oh they did darken his spirit,
When that he was brought over
From ruin and from that great stroke,
From redshanks[185] that were there,
When that a while he was at home,
He did forget his tears.
Oh you great aldermen and sheriffs,
You Lord Mayor also,
That have been in the city, you
Have Gideon overflown.
For your entertainments and your baits
His spirit have so smothered
That he cannot go for a Christ

Whom before he did honour.
O aldermen, O that you had
Considered he was flesh
You would not have so nourished him
And brought forth your relish,
Which was a relish to proud flesh
Which shall crumble to dust,
For truly it hath in him and you,
Raised up fleshly lust.
Oh tremble ye therefore, for you
Have roasted meat so dry;
His wines you did mingle, whereby
You have blinded his eyes.

Much more she uttered in her song, which the relator could not take, the press and noise of people in the chamber swallowing the voice of her words, that they could not be distinctly understood. After which she proceeded to prayer, wherein were delivered, besides many other, the passages following.

O poor soldiers, take heed that you never draw your sword against the saints; do not smite with your tongue, as they did against Jeremiah![186] Oh poor soldiers, why do you appear against those, you have had their breath, their tears, their prayers! Do you think they are against you, when they would take you out of your quagmires, when they tell you you are upon slippery places? They would not rest night nor day [Isaiah 62.6] for you; and will you now mock them, who are for the design for the Lord Jesus? Will you now speak that against them, which you would have bit your tongue in the field, rather than to have spoken? Do not the hearts of those pity you, that you think are against you? If you draw spears against them, they will draw nothing but faith and Christ against you, and can you then stand? Oh no, you will fall backward. When they came to seek Jesus and take him, they could not look upon him, but fell backward [John 18.6]; Jesus Christ set his face like a flint [Isaiah 50.7] against his enemies for you, that he might take you up and crown you, that so you might stand for him. Oh, the lion of the tribe of Judah [Revelation 5.5] calls upon you, will you not hear the voice of the lion? Do men affright you to make you stoop and bow to them; oh here is the voice of the lion of the tribe of Judah, he will lend you privileges, your golden cups [Revelation 14.4] and brave things you have in the earth; oh Lord Jesus come quickly [Revelation 22.20]. Do thou tell them what a lion thou art. Oh, Lord thou wilt not honour them with the great things thou hast for thine that shall reign with thee. Oh that they would repent, that they would

look with pale faces upon him. — Thy servant will leave a testimony
within these walls, this palace,[187] against them, for that they have jeered
against the kingdom and reign of Jesus Christ.

Oh you sergeants![188] Then your hearts shall tremble to put forth your
hand against one of the prophets, or people of the Lord; must you, sergeants, that have prophesied and prayed with the people of the Lord, now
put forth your hand against them? Come Lord Jesus and fill them with
trembling, and let them rather feed upon crusts, than to hold their places
under these men. Know that the glorious time is coming, when that
blessed tribe of Judah shall come in, what will become then of the swift
motions of your feet, where you have run for them that build calves in
Bethel [1 Kings 12.28]. Oh when the glory of that thy people shall appear,
what language shall then come up; oh! you will say, If that were coming
it were well, but will you make no preparation for it? If you will not stand
up for the deliverance of the people, deliverance shall come, though we
know not from whence. If thou art afraid to go into the King's palace,
thou shalt be ashamed when that day cometh. The Lord is bringing about
a glorious freedom, let them know that the time is drawing on, that your
staff of beauty and bonds that have been broken, the Lord will bring them
together again, and they shall be stronger than they were before — Lord,
thou wilt suddenly come to thy temple, the foolish virgins[189] shall then
cry, but says the Lord, I have an open gate only for mine that have oil in
their lamps. You great professors, you who are but lamp ones, you shall not
enter in, when he comes; he will not come as a torn, battered, crushed
Jesus, but as a lovely King, as one full of favour; though many say, Lo,
here is Christ, and there, but these are deceivers; but oh the children shall
by thy spirit know the countenance of the true Christ, his true breath; his
looks from all painted looks[190] that are upon the earth. Jesus Christ will
not come flashily,[191] but with such a light as shall endure, such a light as
you shall see that all other lights are counterfeit to him; though never so
many languages utter their voices, but when thou comest, thy language
shall be discerned. Many are come forth into the world, but thou sayst,
Try the spirits, my saints. It is not they can try the spirits that have read
many volumes; university men have great knowledge, but they cannot try
the spirits;[192] can those that have the form without the power,[193] that
have great arguments? No, they only can try the spirits that are children
indeed; the other by virtue of their literal knowledge, their own understanding, their own apprehensions, their own light, oh such are taken with
flesh, and say, This is Christ and that is Christ; but thy people will not
only try Ranters, for they are known in the face of the sun,[194] but they
will try whether men be for a crucified Christ that suffered upon the cross,
or a Christ within. Thine indeed are for Christ within them,[195] and they
do love Christ as he suffered at Jerusalem, and manifest within them. Oh,

but thine are too apt to run away from the simplicity of the gospel! Though things be high, yet if they have not a footing in a crucified Christ, in God manifest in the flesh, then let not thine embrace them.

Having with these uttered many other things, she sung of the glory of the New Jerusalem,[196] which escaped the relator's pen, by reason of the lowness of her voice, and the noise of the people; only some pieces were taken here and there, but too broken and imperfect here to relate. After her song, she proceeded again to prayer, wherein she uttered the words following.

It is now much that great ones do not tremble, that they have such greedy minds after things here below, if they did take things into their understanding, lest they should not be entertained at thy table. How do they think, that are in high places, to manage their proceedings aright, if they have not the presence of God with them, if they have prayer and faith against them? O, says Joshua,[197] I will rather have all the armies of the world against me, than want the presence of God! Oh, if they were jealous, that they had many enemies within, then they would do as Joshua did, they would set themselves to seek the Lord, they would say, Come soldiers, let us seek the Lord. Thou hast now put them to the trial, now let them examine whether their former prayers, promises and declarations came from a legal[198] and slavish, or a gospel, fear, a fear that they should be smitten down to the earth, or a filial fear, a fear that the name of the Lord would fall upon the ground! O, what will become of thy great name? Had you had the name of God in your eyes, then you would have it still; if the true fear of God wrought in you such effects before, why does it not so now? Why are you now so little for the name of the Lord, and so much for your own name? If you had acknowledged my supremacy then in truth, you would acknowledge it now. O, the Lord cannot endure hypocrites! Rational men themselves abhor that which is flattery and dissembling, and what is not from an ingenious frame of spirit, and will not God much more? Now that you come to have fine houses, warm beds, sweetmeats, do you now pay your vows unto the Lord? Oh, let them not side with the crookedness of this generation; let them draw nigh to meet their God. Oh, come, come, when you were trembling ones, praying ones, then Israel exalted you, and delighted in you, and went to God for your sakes; and now you have offended in Baal,[199] you are dead, your spirits are dead; will you not be told of it? You shall be told of it — Come, O you, that are in any authority, in any office, study what you are to do for the Lord; wherein you might redeem the time, wherein you might serve the Lord. Though you have given up your members to serve sin and vanity [Romans 6.13, 19], let the day suffice that you have recreated, sported, filled, feasted yourselves. Now say, Lord, we will be for thee, and he will receive you. If they now set to temple-work, thou wilt say to them thou thoughtest to have taken them away in the wilderness, because they have done thus, and have gone back in the wilderness. Yet the Lord will say to them, as to David, "I accept of it at thy hand, of the thoughts of thy heart, yet thou shalt not build my house" [2 Samuel 7.4; 1 Chronicles 17.4, 22.8]. Pray for your children, that they may not be taken with crowns; nor with the summer's increase, as their fathers have been. O let them not die without a repenting frame of spirit. Oh thou lovest them that confess their sins; true confession of sin will go with an endeavour against it. Or as David said, "I have made the hearts of the righteous sad, and to mourn, and grieve. Oh, that they might say so; Lord I have been a backslider, but I will yet return." Let them not harden themselves, and become accusers against thine; let them not think much to be accounted revolters, when you are so; you shall be called revolters when you are so; when you act like Demas,[200] do you think you shall go untold of it? The Lord will make you to know it by a witness within you. Do thou recall them, they have been a pleasant voice to thy people, but now they have a confused language [Genesis 11.7,9], and chill and cold spirits, thou wilt make them to know it, Lord. If they sin openly, then reprove them openly. Let not thy people fear to reprove them to their face. Let them do that which is just, Father. Shall they run into fiery temptations, and shall we not tell them? They cast out thy people, but thy people will not cast them out; thy people pray that thy might see thy kingdom, and partake of the breath of his nostrils [2 Samuel 22.16; Psalms 18.15; Job 4.9; Isaiah 2.22], and of the brightness of his coming. Is it not pure gospel for thine to tell them that they are gross sinners against free grace, against the Lord Jesus, the Son. Oh, the sun discovers all things;[201] that which is thrown up against the sun, that appears most clearly; the sun will make you known, what you are in secret. Can you stand it out against the Lord himself? Let not them that have given up their names to thee, be found fighters against thee. Shall thine, oh, Lord, be swallowed up? Oh no, thou wilt but hiss [Zechariah 10.8], and armies shall come even from heaven for thine; and then those that do task and seek to lay on the burthen, what shall they do?

Having uttered these, with some other things, concerning the New Jerusalem, she sung forth the further enlargements of her heart in the song following.

He that did wait these things to know,[202]
    that penned was within,
That book concerning thy coming,
    as Potentate and King.
Oh he did mourn till that the lamb
    did come with cheering there,

And said he would open that book,
    and those seals he would tear.[203]
And lay it wide open before,
    that he might read therein,
Concerning songs of Hallelujah,
    which shall fill to the brim,
And that he should read there also
    the downfall of the whore
Of Babylon [Revelation 17], which sure shall fall,
    and sink within her gore.
And that he also there should read,
    the downfall of the great Gog,
Gog and Magog,[204] how they shall go,
    and by Christ down be plucked.
And he must read also how thou
    wouldst search all nations wide,
And gather in thy remnant there [Micah 2.12; Jeremiah 23.3;
        Revelation 12.17],
    and others wash with tide.
With floods that should rise upon them,
    and make them sink for ever,
That so thy Sion might thee praise,
    who art that high one, rather.
Then that they should exalt the praise
    of men and things on earth
For they know what thou dost declare
    and what thou dost discover.
And John he read long since thereof
    concerning the great fall,[205]
Of those that stood out against him
    who is the chief of all.
Oh he read here, thou wouldst dry up
    Euphrates that river,
And make dry land for thine to go [Revelation 16.12],
    and thither to appear
Before thy throne where they should be
    and abide for evermore.
Therefore John read how that thou wouldst
    the earth again restore.
None shall hinder them from those thrones
    which John there did declare,
Oh a sea of glass there crystal was [Revelation 4.6]
    which none could it compare:

But oh your standing on the earth,
    on glass that brittle is,
Which shall crumble under your feet
    when that there comes forth this,
This sea of glass which is indeed,
    that where thine thee behold;
Oh they may look up unto thee,
    and thorough it extol
Thy love that did a book write sweet,[206]
    and many things there in store
Of royalties which should come out,
    and be given more and more,
Unto those that deny thy foes,
    and Antichrist also,
They that go forth to strike at him,
    thou wilt upon them blow;
Thy spirit upon them shall come forth
    and Antichrist shall fall
Both in person, and also too,
    in his coming principal.[207]
Oh it is Lord, then sweet surely,
    to read of such things here,
And John be mourned abundantly,
    that th' mystery might draw near,
That New Jerusalem above,
    might come down here below,
And that they might see their High,
    when that forth he doth go.

Here she ceased, and lay silent for the space of some two or three hours, until about eight of the clock in the evening, the company being all departed, excepting about four or five persons, she coughed, and being asked by a friend or two, with the relator, how she did, with two or three such like questions, she answered in a very few words (this being the first time the relator had speech with her) and suddenly was carried out in singing, and afterwards in prayer, wherein the relator left her about ten o'clock in the night, speaking to God.

The day following being the seventeenth day of the month, and the last day she spake in Whitehall, she begun with prayer, wherein she was very large, and amongst many other, she uttered the things following.

Though they (*speaking of the soldiers*) may build tabernacles, and may strengthen their cords [Isaiah 54.2], yet thou art risen. O poor creatures, that they should have no heart to hear. O Lord, they are given up to blindness, they will refuse to hear, they will turn and go away. Blessed Father, wilt not thou follow them and shake them? Though they may shake off faith and prayer, yet they shall not shake off thee; oh when the handwriting is come up in their veins, will not their knees smite together? They shall see that an evil heart is in them, and that godliness is another thing than they thought on; though they speak of light, yet they shall know that they are darkness, for they act nothing but darkness, discover nothing but vileness and evil, that such creatures should live in a time of so much mercy, and trample them under feet, wilt not thou reckon with them? Dost not thou reckon with the nations throughout the whole earth? And wilt thou suffer them to go unreckoned with? It is not everyone that hath a tongue to speak great things of thee, that are thy friends; for if it were so, this nation would be full of excellent ones, oh but their heart is deceitful. When Ananias and Sapphira did lie against the Holy Ghost, they were struck dead [Acts 5.1-10]; oh but how often have they lied against the Holy Ghost, and yet thou forbearest; oh thy servant will not let thee alone till thou risest.

Up in thy glory and thy majesty, thou wilt make some to rise that are feeble, poor, low creatures to utter forth against the wise ones of the world; oh they have not thy sap, thy spirit, whatever they pretend. Wilt not thou come forth and confound their language?[208] Oh! thou wilt say, What have you to do to take the name of God in your mouths, when you act for your bellies? If all thine should hold their peace, thou wilt come thyself and appear against them. Oh they shall be called the Jeroboams of the earth, they have made Israel to sin;[209] oh they would not be called Jeroboam, but the Israel of God, and therefore poor Israel is bowed under them, and drawn under their skirts; when Ephraim offended in Baal, then he died in spirit [Hosea 13.1], in the affections of thine. Oh then they will come off with a great deal of damage and rust. Oh that they might now be ashamed, now whiles they are peeping in at the crevice, let them see their abominations; oh take them aside, and tell them they ought not to do so; let them not go and assume that to them, which belongs to God; tell them thou wilt make them to smart and feel thy rod for it. If they had stooped to the powers before, the sin would not have been so great; but to stoop to those powers that have appeared against the Lord Jesus, oh, who can be silent and hold their peace at this? Thou wilt pour out thy spirit upon sons and daughters [Joel 2.28], and they shall witness for thee against them. Thine may be lambs and sheep, meek and lowly; yet they shall be, as thou hast said, as a young lion, and shall tear all that rise up against them [Ezekiel 19.1-9; Hosea 5.14] — Oh, where is thy voice, Lord, thou that speakest with a mighty alarm, and thy voice breaks the cedars [Psalm 29.5]? Oh, thy voice comes forth with much power! Oh, let that voice come forth concerning restauration, and generation-work![210] Oh,

thou hast put a price into the hand of thine, and they have no mind to it!
You show yourselves to be very low; the prophets of old were willing to
look to the Lord, and he sent fiery chariots round about them [2 Kings
2.11]. Oh, if thine would go forth, who should be able to stand before that
wisdom and spirit by which they speak — Everlasting burning shall come
forth in righteousness against you that have put your shoulders to a power
that is against the Lord. Shall they go about to rear up that, which thou
hast said fights positively against the crown of the Lord Jesus? It is not like
the other, for them thou hast taken out of the way; but oh, these have
raked up their honour out of the grave. If you will have a resurrection of
it again, you shall have prayer against you; and the voice of the Lord shall
come forth against you. They think if they could get nations on their side,
then they were well enough! Oh but thou wilt scatter the nations [Jere-
miah 13.24], thou wilt overturn them, and do they think they can hinder
thine overturnings? Thine can rejoice, though they mourn to see poor
Israel cheated and cozened by them, the spirit blasphemed by them, they
can mourn for the sin of the daughter of thy people [Lamentations 4.6];
yet they can rejoice, for New Jerusalem is coming forth through all this.
Thou wilt go on, Lord, and strike down all their inventions, though they
have a great company of great headpieces together; yet a little true wisdom
shall break down all their policy. What is all their wisdom, if they have
not thy fear, thy spirit among them? Thou hast told them plainly, but they
cannot abide to hear it, that the wisdom of the wise shall perish [1 Corinthians 1.19]; and thy poor and contemptible ones shall carry on thy work
for thee in the world; the time is coming that they shall be fruit, that they
shall bring forth no more fruit for thine. They pretend they will do great
things for thee and thine. Oh, but if the eyes were not blinded, they
might see the partiality that is in them! Here is one, no sooner were the
powers put to him, but he took them. Oh, poor creature, how hast thou
deceived us? If thou hast free grace, that must be admired indeed in thee!
Oh but thou shalt have no more, for he will not honour thee any more.
The people of the Lord cry to the Lord against thee, though thou wast a
sweet perfume and a lovely song to the people of the Lord, yet they do not
know how to speak for thee; and if all should come forth, and own thee,
yet thy servant will never do it, she cannot do it, for the work is on foot,
and it is not men nor devils can stop it. When thine take a view of thy
great works in the nation, how thou hast taken away them that made the
nation nauseous and stinking and did build up Babylon, shall now refined
ones come and build up Babylon again? Oh thy love to thy handmaid will
not let her alone, but she must cry unto thee, if thou lovest thy saviour
then stand up, it is no matter if that be laid aside and cast into the dungeon. There are a great many whose god is their belly [Philippians 3.19],[211]
and they are willing to be silent; oh but you saints, do you go and speak

to such as would shut this open door, as is open to the sheep [John 10.7].
— Do you thus requite the Lord who laid down his life for you? O soldiers,
you said you acted for Christ and his flock, oh but your heart is deceived,
and hath turned you aside. Come you mockers, you army men that are
mockers, the Lord saith your bonds shall be made strong, you do add to
the strength of that promise and vow-breaking which went before; you
sometimes said, Let us have the prayers of poor saints, and now you can
take turns in your galleries,[212] and say they are yours, you have fought for
them; is it so? Who gave you your life, and fought for you? Was it not the
Lord Jesus? It is not yours, but the poor's and thy people's, the Lord will
cast you out; and whereas you were expected to be oaks, full of shelter, of
fruits and of refreshing, oh but you have been but blustering oaks, without
root, without sap.

Oh let thine be ashamed, that they have so much looked upon man,
which today is, and tomorrow withers [Matthew 6.30]. Oh thy people suffer even for their own sin; for they have made idols of men; and thou sayst
thou wilt not give thy glory to graven images, and now thou wilt make
thine to smart for it, and to smart a while; were it not for thine, that they
shall be purged and purified to make them ashamed, and lay them in the
dust, to mould them into thy fashion, and to take away their sour leaven
[1 Corinthians 5.8], were it not for this work, thou wouldst make these to
crumble ere a day come to an end; the Assyrian[213] must be burned, when
thou hast done thy work upon Mount Sion. All you great ones, you shall
not at all fare the better for these manifestations of grace which the Lord's
people shall have; oh that you might be humbled at the last breath; was
there ever any laden with so many mercies, and yet so much tin and dross
[Isaiah 1.25] found in them? Oh poor soldiers, your error was here, that
while you did strike down the Philistine without,[214] you have not been
watchful to draw your swords against that that is within; here you were
not inquisitive, and this hath made you to fall so flat, and this hath dead-
ened you. Thou wouldst have thine full of eyes; poor soldiers, you have
had eyes without, but not, as those creatures recorded [Revelation 4.8],
have you had eyes within. — Lord, they can resist the holy one of Israel;
come, can you resist the Lord? You may shoot against the creature's mud
walls, but can you batter the towers of the Lord? Oh poor man, wilt thou
contend with thy maker? How wilt thou contend against so glorious a
King? Dost thou think to come with thy brazen face and jeering countenance against the Lord of glory? Though Christ when he came at first was
willing to become weak, and to be thrown into the grave, but he will
come in flames of fire; you soldiers, he will come as the messenger of his
temple. — Oh poor creatures, this wine of the earth will inflame your
blood, but oh that you might have the wine from above, then would you
be beautified, and then would he say, *Well done, good and faithful servant*

[Matthew 25.21]. — O thy servant is come near that council,[215] and thy servant will pray that they might see and hear, and be delivered from that great fury that is coming forth. Oh soldiers, can you stand against the sword of the Lord [Judges 7.18,20], that great shield? Can you pierce the breastplate that is from on high? Oh, the saints are able to fight with you, not with material weapons, but with the sword of faith and the spirit; oh where is the sword of Goliah[216] that can come and fight against that? Oh poor soldiers, the Lord hath sent his servant to tell you of your wickedness, and to tell you what hath been done in Scotland, Ireland,[217] and elsewhere: if you keep not chronicles, others do; the Lord hath written them down, and he will bring them forth. — Thou hast a controversy with all languages, and they only that have the language of Canaan [Isaiah 19.18] shall be taken into thy Canaan, and shall have the honey drops there. They cannot believe such great things are coming out, as the reign of Jesus Christ; that thou art staining the pride of all glory, and that thou wilt have no more monarchies till the monarchy of Christ come forth. It is because they are so much seeking one from another, they are so taken up and wrapped up in their own mantles, that they have no eyes to look up for Elias his mantle [2 Kings 2.8]. They have the spirit of man, and the courage of man. But what is all that courage? says Elihu, I have seen that for all that, ages should teach wisdom, and years give understanding [Job 32.7]; yet you could not bring forth an answer in wisdom to the condition of Job;[218] so I waited for others, and was afraid myself to speak, until the spirit came upon me [Job 32.12], then I was carried forth to speak beyond my own courage. Oh thy spirit is above the spirit of man; thy spirit informs and teacheth, and brings forth new things, and declares old things; thy spirit brings forth what the ways of men are, it doth declare the great overturnings and disappointments that men shall meet with; when thou openest, who can shut [Isaiah 22.22; Revelation 3.8]? It is not all their jealousies and surmisings concerning designings, and this and the other thing, it is not all these things that can stop the pipes of Christ that are golden; can you hinder the oil that runs so sweet [Zechariah 4.12]? Blessed be thy name for that glorious privilege that thine have, they are made partakers of thine anointing, and he calls them fellows; oh they are poor mortals that he should call them fellows! Oh some poor creatures call themselves Christ; because of this oneness with Christ, they will have no distinguishing, thou wilt make them to know that there is a difference between head and members.[219] There is a wicked generation that are risen up about this place that do say so, that do pretend many spiritual things, who are enemies to Jesus; others come out more openly, others more secretly, how are they ready to join their evil spirit with the spirit of the Lord Jesus? Thy servant sometimes contended against them near this place, and now she is come to bear a greater testimony against them;

when thy sweet wine comes forth, and thy spirit is poured out, then they bring in their false wine; oh but it shall never enter into thy treasury, where thine are; they say they (*speaking of some rude spirits which came to hear her*) are one spirit with thy servant, but thy servant abhors it through the spirit of that crucified Jesus.[220] — This that thou hast now done upon thy servant, they will not understand that it is an intimation to them of the pouring out of thy spirit upon thine own, wherein they shall go forth against the world. Thy servant was one that was simple, an idiot, and did not study in such things as these, and must thy servant now float upon the mighty and broad waters (*meaning of the spirit*)? Thou saidst indeed that thy servant should declare in Gath and publish in Askelon.[221] They will say the spirit of madness and distraction is upon her, and that it is immodesty; but thou knowest, Lord, that it is thy spirit; for thou hast cast thy servant where she would not, and hast taken her contrary to all her thoughts; surely thou shalt be glorified and advanced by it; it is the Lord that comes, and enlarges, and fills with his spirit, and lays his foundation with precious stones [Revelation 21.19–20] and sparkling colours. Thy servant would not have any take it in without trial; let them try whether it is from thy spirit, or from what it is. Oh thy servant knows it is from thy spirit; let them know that it is so too, by the language of it, by the rule through which it comes; how is the written word carried forth in it? Thy spirit takes the scripture all along, and sets the soul a-swimming therein; oh, those things that are concealed are made manifest, when thy spirit comes forth; oh that they might know what is the true fountain, and what is puddled water! Wilt thou dip them, Father, in the spiritual baptism? This baptism of fire [Matthew 3.11; Luke 3.16] cleanseth, zeal Is another thing than a passionate humour: where true zeal is, there the flame of the Lord is; there is much in nature that may deceive. A fine curious nature may seem to be grace, which is not; an amiable carriage and good words, these are all nature. Tell the sons of Issachar [Genesis 46.13; 1 Chronicles 7.1] that go forth to the work of the Lord, what qualifications, what manner of conversations should be in them, and in the world, suitable to such a day as this; this is a day wherein thou callest up thine to glorify thee in the fires, or that the names "courtier" and "king" should never come up again; and though there be now a finer name yet there is the same thing, the same superfluity and vanity as was among the kings of old; they come forth in sheep's clothing [Matthew 7.15]. You council, you think you have done well in this, but surely the passing bell shall ring for you. This is the saddest day that ever poor England had; formerly their children had their black patches, and naked necks, and powdered locks, and so it is now;[222] kings must then sit alone, and so they do now. What, David! Thou whom I have raised up from the lowest of men, from the dust [Psalm 113.7–8; 1 Samuel 2.8], wilt thou do this? These are crying things that are come up in thine ears, oh Lord; how can they be fit to rule and judge a nation, to reprove sin in a nation, when they cannot rule, and judge, and reprove their own families?[223] They that will not hear of their sins, they shall feel of the smart thereof, that is, the sins they are galled within their conscience, but it was not so with David. For when Nathan told him of his sin, he struck upon his breast and mourned [2 Samuel 12.13]. — Though the name of Gideon was upon him (*speaking of the supreme magistrate*) in the field, yet now it is taken off from him, thou shalt no more be called valiant, because thou canst not be contented with the name of thy righteous ones; therefore thy name shall not be long. As to the name "general", thou hast, Lord, been with him, and hast showed him thy presence. But in thy other name, where is thy victory, thy righteousness, thy zeal, thy love, thy conquest now? Will not the Lord shut thee out, thou that goest about to shut out the saints? The Lord will shut out thee. It is a King, not saints, but King Jesus that thou hast sought to shut out; hadst not thou better to have died in the field, to have fallen in thy tent, than to come into this great palace which the Lord will rent from thee?[224] Oh that he might be wrung out from among them, that he might not seek the living among the dead [Luke 24.5]. He seeks to do living actions, and says he is not against us, but for us. How can he do any living things among dead men, dead things? Does not he confound himself in his own language? Do not his actions fly in his face? Does not his conscience say, Thou tongue [Psalms 52.4, 120.3], thou sayst not right? Tell him Lord God, though he thinks he is so wise, and others about him, yet tell him they are taken in their own wisdom [Psalms 10.2, 59.12; Proverbs 6.2, 11.6], they do not think what a poison it will become unto them. Art thou a rational man, a wise and a valiant soldier? How can the commonalty be relieved, and[225] thou hast such great things for thy table? Wars shall come out against other nations, and what will you do then for pay, soldiers? Oh you old prophets! that you should applaud him, and be chaplains to him! I tell you the Lord God will eclipse your glory, he will put a stammering speech into you, you shall not suck from God's wine cellars, the Lord will not bring so much as a taste of his wine to you. You have turned his wine into water [John 2.1–11], will you sow your down pillows of flesh under his elbows? Hast not thou a great deal to reckon with them for that greatness they have had above all other men? He hath now a greater controversy with you than he had before; you amended the matter well indeed, when you gathered up a magistracy that might uphold you, when you must both fall down into the ditch [Matthew 15.4; Luke 6.39]. The Lord hath said that "both prophet and priest, and all that have cleaved together, they shall fall" [Jeremiah 23.11]. You will say, Why do you call us priests? Indeed thy servant would not call you so, it is a grief to her heart;

but you do their actions, and will not you be likened to them? You will
not hear; you will say, Do you think to contradict us who are wise, great
scholars, and university men? Yea Lord, thou wilt make a poor silly creature to come out against them, because they have acted so sillily, and thou
Lord wilt now take away their glory out of this nation. You will say you
are not to meddle with the powers, but who meddles more than you, who
have provoked the magistrate to this, and have helped to lead them into
the pit? If you were the Daniels[226] of the Lord, you would not care for the
king's portion, as you do. Oh poor clergy! You have put off the outward
badge of Antichrist, and you have retained the inward. What is become of
your zeal and exaltations of Christ, have you ever a New Covenant sermon[227] to bring to your great ruler? You will mud it before you come; the
Lord will have it set out in the freeness, and fullness, and glory of it in all
the tendency and fruits of it. Are they like to the sermons of the saints
formerly, to the apostles' sermons which the Lord Jesus brought forth?
More of their own heads and fancies are in it, than of thy dainties; of
their flowers, than of thine. Thou dost not, Lord, look at the curious deck-
ing of the dishes. No, thou lookest at the meat in it. Flowers will soon
wither, and their fine adornings will come to nothing; but the true meat,
that will abide for ever [John 6.27]. Lord, rouse the poor clergy; thy servant is persuaded some of them are thy dear ones; wilt thou bring up them
as thy great alarm to battle? Let their trumpet sound forth, not with such
an uncertain sound [1 Corinthians 14.8] as they do, but with a complete
sound, that we may prepare to the battle, to stand, appear, and go forth
for the Lord. If you bring forth true salt, then all unsavoury salt shall be
discovered by it; the unsavoury salt now comes in, which is fit neither for
the land, nor for the dunghill [Luke 14.34–35]. — Hear oh house of Israel,
you clergy, and oh house of the king! Why is thy servant come forth in
thy spirit to proclaim your sin, and lay open your iniquity, and is not this
to be considered by you? Oh, you cannot abide to think it comes from
God; for then you would tremble; they say, We will not own it to be from
God, but from some evil spirit, some witchcraft, some design or hiring of
men. But oh! says God, though you would not acknowledge it, yet you
shall acknowledge it. Says the Lord, I would have it come against you at
your first entering in; those of the clergy that are about you, they do not
speak plainly, and faithfully against you; therefore the Lord hath sent a
poor handmaid into the palace, and there she shall declare it, and though
you will not come yourselves, yet your servants shall declare it to you, and
it shall be left upon the beams and walls of this house against you. I have
brought my word into thy place, thy very palace,[228] and it shall enter the
very walls and hangings thereof against thee; and at such a time, Lord, as
now, if not now, it would not have been suffered. For when they had got

in their great body, then she must not have spoken here, that they might see, that it is thou, Lord, that makes a cry to come out against their transgression. The Lord would have your protestations, vows, covenants and narrations brought into your palace against you, this shall be bitterness in your dishes. You shall have plenty and fullness, but without comfort.

*Here she begun and continued her
song, much whereof the relator did
take, and was as follows.*

Blessed be thy name oh thou Lord,
Which wilt break forth herein,
Thou wilt declare thy glory bright,
Against all them that sin.
Enemies shall know their folly great,
Which prayer and songs do show,
When songs and melody come forth,
Thy wind[229] shall on them blow.
A wind Lord, that shall enter in,
Into their palaces great,
A blustering wind from the great God,
A whirlwind that's complete.
That will tear them up by the roots,
And cast them on the ground,
Where they no greenness shall have here,
No sap shall be there found.
Oh clergy that you should so wrong,
And extenuate your joy,
By bringing forth unto proud man,
That which God doth not convoy.
Oh that you should so nurture them,
And cheer them in their sin,
I tell you that Christ for this will
Not make your souls to sing.
You shall not hear Sion's songs so sweet [Psalm 137.3],
Nor their mirth which draws nigh,
But when it cometh forth to light,
You suddenly shall die.
Oh when that harmony comes out,
In the reign of a Christ,
Oh then you clergy shall go down,
And in it have no interest.

Oh when those dear streams from on high,
Come running out so clean,
They shall not enter into you,
Who in the dirt have lain.
But they shall float and spring forth on
The grounds that lovely are,
Oh they shall have the sweet springings
From the Lord, who is so rare.
They that would not any baulk here,
But openly declare,
Oh it is they shall come to him,
Whom nothing can compare.
For they that zealous have been for
A Christ, as Lord and King,
He will himself open their mouth,
And make them for to sing.
Oh therefore come! Oh come thou Christ!
Oh show thyself now here,
Oh come! come King Jesus, declare
How thou art drawing near.
And that thine may from Sodom[230] go,
And follow thee throughout,
Their travels in those pleasant plains
Do thou compass about.
And that flesh may thine fly before,
That darkness may go out,
And that King Jesus he may come,
And there himself set out.
The Lord is gone forth mightily,
He all might doth appear;
Oh come, oh come you enemies,
The great God for to fear.
Oh tremble and astonished be,
To hear that he draws on,
Against you he comes forth apace,
The oppressors of the land.
Oh he hath said that he will reign,
Therefore rulers shall fly,
Oh he hath said that he'll cast out
The fourth great monarchy.[231]
Oh he will show unto the pure,
And such that are upright,

To manifest to these proud walls,
That now to you are in sight.
Oh therefore clergy, and you state,
Nothing at all you shall,
When that the Lord Christ he doth speak,
You utterly shall fall.
What will you do then that have not
That wisdom which is good,
And how will you abide that stroke,
And that eternal flood.
Oh how can you then say you stand
For those that are Christ's flock,
When that you do so much declare,
So much for this great oak?
Oh can you then stand out and say,
Oh will you not then stammer,
To hear the Lord, and also to
See his most glorious banner?
Oh but when he cometh, and when
You feel his stroke indeed;
Oh then you shall have no supply,
To comfort in your need.
Many of you shall only have
The earth to feed therein;
But you shall have no sights of him,
Which is that mighty King.
Oh he will rend you throughout,
That lion which is strong,
He will you trample under foot,
Who is my joy and song.

Having sung this song with some enlargement, she breathed forth in prayer; a short account of some things therein you have as follows.

You will say, Have not our eyes seen this before, and have not our ears heard this before? Oh but when thou pourest forth by a vessel that is altogether unlikely that any such liquor should enter into it, though you that are the great ones, whom it concerned, would not lend your ears, yet the Lord hath accomplished his design in this work; and thy servant will leave this in the bosom of them that have heard these beatings of thy spices;[232] and have their senses open to feel the smell thereof. Let thy servant request this of thee, that when she is at a distance, they would hold up a

ready for her. Notwithstanding this weakness, after she had kept her bed eleven days together, without any sustenance at all for the first five days, and with only a little toast in small beer once in twenty-four hours for the rest of the time, she rose up in the morning, and the same day travelled on foot from Whitehall to Hackney, and back to Mark Lane in London, in health and strength.

FINIS

COMMENTARY

In the preparation of these notes, the following texts have been those relied on most consistently: Capp, *Fifth Monarchy Men*; *Calendar of State Papers: Domestic* (hereafter *CSPD*), *Dictionary of National Biography* (hereafter *DNB*), *Biographical Dictionary of British Radicals*, ed. Greaves and Zaller; Woolrych, *Commonwealth to Protectorate*. Other sources are given full references in the notes themselves.

1   *The Cry of a Stone:* the title refers to the apocryphal Second Book of Esdras (Wiseman, "Unsilent Instruments," 186), also known as "the Apocalypse of Ezra" or *4 Ezra*, a Jewish apocalypse not preserved in rabbinic tradition, but known thanks to its popularity in Christian churches: see *The Anchor Bible Dictionary*, ed. David Noel Freedman, 2 vols. (New York and London: Doubleday, 1992), 2: 611. The middle chapters of 2 Esdras comprise seven revelations granted to Ezra in Babylon, several in the form of visions. The first vision concerns the seer's "bewilderment and grief that a righteous God should allow his people to suffer at the hands of a nation that knows him not ... The angel Uriel ... informs him that the end of the present age is approaching and will at last come when the number of the righteous is fulfilled. In chapter 5 he is shown signs and wonders which will herald the approach of the end" (D. S. Russell, *The Method and Message of Jewish Apocalyptic* [London: SCM Press, 1964], 63–64). One of these "signs and wonders" is that voiceless stones will prophesy:

> But if the Most High grant thee to live, thou shalt see that which is after the third kingdom to be troubled; and the sun shall suddenly shine forth in the night, and the moon in the day: and blood shall drop out of wood, and the stone shall give his voice, and the peoples shall be troubled ... (2 Esdras 5.4–5)

2   *January 1653:* by the modern (Gregorian) calendar, this is January
    1654. Since the latter part of the twelfth century, 25 March (Lady
    Day) had, for legal and official purposes, been the first day of the year,
    hence Trapnel's references to January and February as the eleventh
    and twelfth months; however, many people continued to calculate the
    new year from 1 January, and usage was not regularised until the adop-
    tion of the Gregorian calendar in 1752. Consequently many seven-
    teenth-century texts double-date the months of January and February,
    encompassing both calendars. BL (published in the same year as CUL)
    changes this reference to 1654, though it does not amend "eleventh
    month" to "first month." I have retained the original dates from the
    copy-text.
3   *wise virgins in Sion:* a reference to Matthew 25.1–13; see note 189.
4   *pretends:* professes or claims (with no implication of feigning).
5   *scribes:* the scribes were Jewish authorities on the Law of God, who
    were responsible for administering it to the people. They were associ-
    ated with a rigid legalism; it is thus used here as a term of disparage-
    ment.
6   *the seventh day of the eleventh month:* the dates and duration of
    Trapnel's trance in Whitehall are difficult to determine with any
    certainty. The information we are given in *The Cry of a Stone*, some
    of it conflicting, is as follows:

    a) the trance lasted from 7 January to 19 January (p. 4). However, 7
    January 1645 was a Saturday, a day on which the Council of State,
    which was examining Powell, did not meet (Woolrych, *Commonwealth
    to Protectorate*, 388).
    b) 7 January is given as "the sixth day of the week," that is, a Friday,
    whereas the Friday was 6 January. This suggests the likelihood of 6
    January, not 7, as the first day of Trapnel's trance.
    c) the trance is said variously to have lasted twelve days (p. 4), or
    eleven days and twelve nights (p. 78).
    d) there is general agreement that there are transcripts of seven or
    eight days of prophesying (pp. 3, 5, 16).
    e) the relator tells us (p. 16) that he began his record on 10 January,
    and that Trapnel spoke for the last time on 17 (not, as suggested
    above, 19) January (p. 66).

    The first published account of Trapnel's Whitehall trance, *Strange
    and Wonderful Newes from White-hall* (hereafter *SWN*), published in
    March 1654, and on which *The Cry of a Stone* (CS) clearly draws, par-
    ticularly in the opening and closing pages, offers the following rele-
    vant information:

a) Powell's examination is given as "the 7 day of the 11 month called *Ianu.* being the 6 day of the week, or Fryday" (p. 3). As we have already seen, the Friday was not the 7th, but the 6th. The naming of the day as "Fryday" strengthens the possibility of Friday the 6th being the day Trapnel fell into her trance.

b) the relator began recording on 10 January (erroneously given as February here, but still referred to as the eleventh month) (p. 6). This accords with the date given in *The Cry of a Stone.*

On the basis of this evidence, I would suggest the following as the likeliest calendar of events: Powell's examination took place on Friday 6 January (*SWN*, p. 3). Trapnel fell into her trance at midday, took to her bed in Mr Roberts's ordinary at 11.00 p.m. (*SWN*, p. 3; *CS*, p. 4), and began prophesying on Saturday 7 January. There were three days with no record (Saturday, Sunday and Monday), or four if the Friday is also counted (*CS*, p. 5). The relator began transcribing her words on Tuesday 10 January (the fourth day, or fifth if the Friday is counted) (*SWN*, p. 6; *CS*, p. 16); he continued recording until Tuesday 17 January, when Trapnel finished speaking, making eight days of the relator's account, and eleven days and twelve nights of the trance (*SWN*, pp. 3, 8; *CS*, pp. 4, 78). She then slept, and walked home in the morning (*SWN*, p. 8; *CS*, p. 79) on Wednesday 18 January.

I have been unable to corroborate Friday 6 January as the date of Powell's examination at Whitehall. *DNB* and Edward Rogers (*Some Account of the Life and Opinions of a Fifth-Monarchy Man. Chiefly Extracted from the Writings of John Rogers, Preacher* [London: Longman, Green, Reader and Dyer, 1867]) record him as preaching against the government on 19 December, being detained on 21 December and released on 24 December, again preaching against Cromwell on Christmas Day, and a new order for his arrest being given on 10 January; Rogers says that he also preached against the government on 9 January in a church in Newgate market. These accounts suggest that orders for detention followed swiftly on anti-government preaching, and that it is unlikely that Powell did not preach between 25 December and 9 January. If my calendar of events is correct, it sems likely he preached and was detained in the week leading up to Friday 6 January, was released, preached again on Monday 9 January, and was rearrested on 10 January.

The end-date of Trapnel's trance of 19 January given by both *SWN* and *CS* seems to be erroneous. *CS* draws heavily on *SWN* in its opening and closing sections, and perhaps thus reproduced the date without checking whether it fitted in with the other dates it gives (which, of course, it does not). The inconsistencies can probably be accounted for by the rapid preparation of the texts for the press.

7   *Mr Powell:* Vavasor Powell was a prominent Welsh Baptist/Fifth Mon-
    archist preacher, who had been a chaplain in the Parliamentary army.
    In the early 1650s he was a key figure in the Commission for the Pro-
    pagation of the Gospel in Wales and an important influence on
    Major-General Thomas Harrison (see note 50). Like many others,
    Powell was a supporter of the Barebones Parliament, and, in the days
    following the declaration of Cromwell as Lord Protector, preached
    frequently against the new turn of events and in particular against the
    apostate Cromwell, for which he was repeatedly arrested and released;
    it was at his examination by the Council of State following one such
    arrest in January 1654 that Trapnel spoke the prophecies published in
    The Cry of a Stone. The precise date of the hearing is difficult to deter-
    mine; see note 6 above. Powell preached again at Christ Church,
    Newgate (where Christopher Feake was minister; see note 14) on 9
    January, and was rearrested on 10 January.

8   *the council now sitting in Whitehall:* the Council of State was at this
    time the chief executive body. It had been established on 13 February
    1649 following the execution of the king on 30 January; its members
    were to be elected annually by, and predominantly from among, MPs.

9   *Mr Roberts:* a William Roberts is recorded as a member of the Com-
    pany of Innholders in 1651; see *London Citizens in 1651. Being a Tran-
    script of Harleian Ms. 4778*, ed. J. C. Whitebrook (London: A. W.
    Cannon and Co., 1910), 8.

10 *ordinary:* an eating house or tavern.

11 *Colonel Sydenham ... Mr Birkenhead:* William Sydenham, William
    West, John Chetwood, Robert Bennett, John Bingham, Francis Lang-
    don, Hugh Courtney and Henry Birkenhead had all been members of
    the recently dissolved Barebones Parliment; Sydenham was also a
    member of the Council of State. The presence of these public figures
    at Trapnel's prophesying indicates the extraordinarily high level of in-
    terest in the event. Later in the year, Trapnel stayed in the houses of
    Colonel Bennett and his wife, and of Captain Langdon and his wife,
    when she was sent by her congregation to prophesy in Cornwall. For
    her account of this journey, see *Anna Trapnel's Report and Plea* (1654)
    and her *A Legacy for Saints* (1654).

12 *Captain Bawtrey:* untraced.

13 *Mr Lee:* perhaps the puritan divine Samuel Lee (1625–91). He was
    made minister of St Botolph's, Bishopsgate, by Cromwell, a position
    he occupied until August 1659.

14 *Mr Feake the minister:* Christopher Feake was minister of Christ Church,
    Newgate, from 1649, and lecturer at St Anne's, Blackfriars and at All-
    hallows the Great, Thames Street (on "lecturers," see Christopher

Hill, *God's Englishman: Oliver Cromwell and the English Revolution* [London: Weidenfeld and Nicolson, 1970], 46–48). He was one of the most prominent Fifth-Monarchist leaders in London from 1651 to 1660, urging radical measures on the Barebones Parliament, with whom he quickly became disillusioned. He was frequently imprisoned through the 1650s. Unlike many Fifth Monarchists, he was not a Baptist. See note 7.

15 *Lady Darcy and Lady Vermuyden:* Lady Darcy was Mary, second wife of John Savage, Earl Rivers, Baron Darcy of Chiche; Lady Vermuyden was Katherine, wife of Sir Cornelius Vermuyden, a Dutch engineer and confidant of Cromwell. He was a millenarian, enthusiastic for a coalition between Holland and England, the two Protestant commonwealths, as a way to advance the kingdom of Christ. See note 39.

16 *I was trained up to my book and writing:* rates of female literacy are notoriously hard to determine, varying according to social rank and geographical location as well as precise historical moment. It has been estimated that women's literacy rose during the seventeenth century to over 10 percent, whilst in London the figures were perhaps as high as 25 percent early in the century, rising to nearly 50 percent by its end (Anne Laurence, *Women in England 1500–1760: A Social History* [London: Weidenfeld and Nicolson, 1994], 106). Trapnel is likely to have been schooled by her congregation. On literacy, see, too, David Cressy, *Literacy and the Social Order: Reading and Writing in Tudor and Stuart England* (Cambridge: Cambridge University Press, 1980); *Literacy and Social Development in the West: A Reader*, ed. Harvey J. Graff (Cambridge: Cambridge University Press, 1981); Nigel Wheale, *Writing and Society: Literacy, Print and Politics in Britain 1590–1660* (London and New York: Routledge, 1999).

17 *the church-meeting at Allhallows (whereof Mr John Simpson is a member):* John Simpson, a leading Fifth Monarchist in the early 1650s, was a lecturer at the Fifth-Monarchist/Baptist congregation of Allhallows the Great, Thames Street, from 1647–62, and rector of, and lecturer at, St Botolph's, Aldgate, an open Independent/Baptist congregation, from 1652. Simpson had served in the parliamentary army, and by 1647 was a close friend of Henry Jessey (see note 19). The dismissal of the Barebones Parliament turned Simpson against Cromwell; he prophesied against him in December 1653, was arrested on 25 January 1654, and on 28 January he and Feake were imprisoned in Windsor Castle, where he stayed until July (see Trapnel's letter to them there in *A Legacy for Saints* [1654], 57–60). Although his views changed in some respects in later years, he remained consistently hostile to the Protectorate.

18 *Mr Greenhill, preacher at Stepney:* William Greenhill, Independent min-

ister, and formerly a member of the Westminster Assembly. He was appointed Vicar of Stepney in October 1652.

19 *Mr Henry Jessey:* a prominent Particular Baptist and Fifth Monarchist (though close also to the Independents), Jessey joined Feake and Simpson as a lecturer at Allhallows the Great in 1651.

20 *Mr Venning, preacher at Olave's in Southwark:* Ralph Venning, Independent minister and lecturer at St Olave's church, Southwark, where he established his reputation as a preacher.

21 *Mr Knollys:* Hanserd Knollys was a Particular Baptist also interested in Fifth-Monarchist ideas. He gathered a Particular Baptist church in London in 1645, which he led for the rest of his life; petitioned Parliament with Richard Hollaston for the abolition of tithes in 1649 and 1652; and in a letter of 3 April 1657, written with other radical leaders, urged Cromwell not to accept the English crown.

22 *the church of Allhallows in Lime Street:* the church of Allhallows the Great, led by John Simpson, was in Thames Street. The sense here seems to be that the congregation gathered in premises in Lime Street for a day of thanksgiving. There were a number of buildings on Lime Street large enough for a sizeable gathering: the Company of Fishmongers had premises there (Keith Lindley, *Popular Politics and Religion in Civil War London* [Aldershot: Scolar Press, 1997], 168), and there was also Pewterer's Hall, which stood on the west side of Lime Street, one of the city halls later appropriated to the use of the nonconformists in the reign of Charles II. Robert Bragge assembled a congregation at Pewterer's Hall after the Bartholomew ejectment, though he had probably gathered the church before the Restoration. Bragge had settled in the parish of Allhallows the Great, Thames Street, in the late 1640s or early 1650s, where he gathered an Independent congregation (Walter Wilson, *The History and Antiquities of Dissenting Churches and Meeting Houses in London, Westminster, and Southwark, including the Lives of their Ministers, from the Rise of Nonconformity to the Present Time,* 4 vols. [London, 1814], 1: 208–9).

23 *the army that was then drawing up towards the city:* the New Model Army occupied the capital on 6 August 1647, in order to protect Independent interests in Parliament and impeach eleven Presbyterian MPs. See *Puritanism and Liberty: Being the Army Debates (1647–9) from the Clarke Manuscripts with Supplementary Documents,* ed. A. S. P. Woodhouse (London: Dent, 1938; repr. 1974), (23)–(27); Christopher Hill, *The Century of Revolution 1603–1714,* 2nd ed. (Walton on Thames: Nelson: 1980), 95–96; Christopher Hibbert, *Cavaliers and Roundheads: The English at War 1642–1649* (London: BCA/ HarperCollins, 1993), 257–58.

24 *Minories in Aldgate parish:* Trapnel lodged with a Mrs Harlow in the

Minories, a street running from Aldgate High Street to Tower Hill. The street took its name from the *Sorores Minores*, or Little Sisters, an order of nuns founded by St Clare of Assisi in 1215, who established their convent here in 1293. See Edward H. Sugden, *A Topographical Dictionary to the Works of Shakespeare and his Fellow Dramatists* (Manchester: Manchester University Press, 1925), 348; Adrian Room, *The Street Names of England* (Stanford, Eng.: Paul Watkins, 1992), 76.

25 *King of Salem:* i.e., Christ; Salem is another name for Jerusalem.

26 *Hermon Hill:* Mount Hermon is on the eastern boundary of Palestine; see Deuteronomy 4.48; Joshua 12.5, 13.5; Psalms 89.12, 133.3.

27 *vision of horns:* there were many biblical precedents for prophets having visions of horns; see Daniel 7.7; 8.3; Habakkuk 3.4; Zechariah 1.18–19; Revelation 5.6; 12.3; 13.1,11, 17.3,7. For Fifth Monarchists, the prophecies of Daniel were the most signficant: Mary Cary wrote a long interpretation of Daniel 7 as a prophecy of the evil and downfall of Charles I, published as *The Little Horns Doom and Downfall* (1651), and William Aspinwall published his *Explication . . . of the Seventh Chapter of Daniel* (1654) which also identified the "little horn" of the prophecy as Charles I; Feake and Powell preached at Blackfriars on the vision of the horns in Daniel on 19 December 1653. The Fifth-Monarchist focus on Daniel can be explained by the centrality to the book of the realisation of the kingdom of God: "The book as a whole concerns how the rule of God became a reality of this world. . . . Believers under pressure can stand by their convictions sure that the powers that be will ultimately acknowledge where true power lies and who is its witness" (John E. Goldingay, *Word Biblical Commentary*, vol. 30: *Daniel* [Dallas: Word Books,1989], 330). On seventeenth-century understandings of prophecy, see Introduction, pp. xiii–xv, and note 106.

28 *army . . . Southwark-way:* "then came the Army, welcomed by friendly Southwark, entering the City in triumph on 6 August" (David Underdown, *Pride's Purge: Politics in the Puritan Revolution* [Oxford: Clarendon Press, 1971], 83); for the circumstances of this entry, see Underdown, *Pride's Purge*, chap. 4 passim, especially 79–83.

29 *Absalom . . . David:* see 2 Samuel 15. Absalom was David's son. He engineered a coup d'état against his father, having spent many years conspiring against him. He gained people's loyalty by standing at the gate and, when they came seeking judgement from the king concerning a controversy, told them that there was no one to hear them. If he were king, he said, everyone would have access to him. He is thus a model of filial deceit and betrayal.

30 *H.J. and Jo. S.:* probably Henry Jessey and John Spencer; see note 19 and Introduction, p. xvii, note 13.

31 *war with Scotland:* Scotland, where the future Charles II had been rec-
ognised as king, was invaded by the Commonwealth army, with Cromwell as Commander-in-Chief, in 1650. It was during this campaign
that the Declaration of Musselburgh was published by the soldiers and
junior officers; see note 79.

32 *9th of Zechariah, verse 11:* actually Zechariah 9.14. Because she is
quoting from memory, Trapnel's quotations often paraphrase slightly,
as here, the biblical text. The wording of the biblical quotations and
allusions included in *The Cry of a Stone* suggests that Trapnel was familiar with both the King James Bible (1611) and the Geneva Bible
(1560). The earlier version remained popular with Puritans and sectaries because of its Calvinistic marginal notes; see Christopher Hill,
The English Bible and the Seventeenth-Century English Revolution (London: Allen Lane/The Penguin Press, 1993), 56–64.

33 *Gideon:* Gideon was chosen by God to free Israel from the occupying
forces of the Midianites; see Judges 6–8. Cromwell is figured as Gideon
throughout *The Cry of a Stone:* an apt identification in many ways, for
Gideon was a military leader who cast out idol worship and reintroduced the true religion, defeated and banished the Midianites, and yet
who, when offered the crown in recognition of his military triumphs,
refused to become king, on the grounds that it was God alone who
ruled over Israel. The result is a biblical account which emphasises
"the theme of apostasy and its consequences and the over-ruling
power and grace of God in choosing and endowing his agent Gideon
and effecting his purpose almost independently of human agency in
the crisis" (John Gray, *The New Century Bible Commentary: Joshua,
Judges, Ruth* [Basingstoke: Marshall, Morgan and Scott Publications
Ltd., 1986], 205). See Introduction, pp. xxxiii–xxxv.

34 *Dunbar fight:* the Battle of Dunbar, in which the Commonwealth army
beat the Scots, took place on 3 September 1650. Dunbar was seen as
Cromwell's most decisive victory; see Gentles, *The New Model Army
in England, Ireland and Scotland,* 397–98.

35 *Gideon and the lapping ones with him:* see Judges 7.1–8. God tells
Gideon to select for his army to fight the Midianites only those who,
when taken to drink at the river, "lapped, putting their hand to their
mouth." "By the three hundred men that lapped," God tells Gideon,
"will I save you, and deliver the Midianites into thine hand" (Judges
7.6,7). See note 33.

36 *outward man:* the body (as opposed to the soul).

37 *Dr French's wife . . . Mrs Sansom: Dr French's wife* was perhaps the wife
of Dr John French, "one of the two physicians to the whole [parlia-
mentary] army, under the conduct of Sir Tho. Fairfax, knight" (*DNB*,
vol. 7, 691–92). *Mrs Bond* was perhaps the wife of the puritan divine

John Bond, formerly a member of the Westminster Assembly, or perhaps the widow of William Kendall, a merchant active in parish politics in the early 1640s and, later, a member of the City's committee to
receive information on "scandalous and seditious ministers"; he was,
as Trapnel puts it, "for the Presbyterian government'; see Lindley,
Popular Politics and Religion, 67–68, 70–71, 266–67. *Mrs Smith* is untraced. *Mrs Sansom* was perhaps Mary, the wife of Vice-Admiral Robert Sansum; in January 1652–53, during the First Dutch War of 1652–
54, he captured a Flushing man-of-war off Newcastle, and fitted it out
for the state's service.

38 *Mr Ash:* probably Simeon Ash, one of the Cornhill lecturers, and a
member of the Westminster Assembly. He was minister of St Austin's
from 1655–62.

39 *the first great battle:* the First Dutch War lasted from 1652 to 1654. The
Rump Parliament had sought an alliance with the Dutch Republic,
the other main Protestant power in Europe. However, this prospective
alliance was rejected by the Dutch, who, it became clear, were com-
mitted to supporting the House of Stuart. In addition to this rejection,
the Navigation Act was passed in the autumn of 1651, which aimed
to challenge Amsterdam for its key position as commercial centre of
the world. The war that ensued was, then, both a religio-political and
a commercial contest. Fifth Monarchists supported the war both as a
"divine crusade" and on trade grounds: the war benefited cloth-
workers, who were well-represented in the sect. See Capp, *Fifth Monarchy Men*, 153; Woolrych, *Commonwealth to Protectorate*, 277–88.

40 *at Widow Smith's, glazier:* a Thomas Smith is recorded as a member of
the Company of Glaziers (i.e., those whose trade was to glaze win-
dows) in 1651 (*London Citizens in 1651*, ed. Whitebrook, 10). Women
often took over the running of the business after their husbands'
deaths.

41 *Mr Allen . . . Mr Knollys:* John Allen (or Aleyn) (d. 1663) was a Common Councilman for the Ward of Aldersgate Without from 1649–58
and in 1660, and Deputy (i.e., senior Common Councilman for the
Ward) from 1654; he was alderman for the Ward of Billingsgate from
December 1658 until he was discharged (with a fine of £520) in September 1659. Allen was a painter, specialising in heraldic painting; in
1658–59 he entered an agreement with John Withy, Henry Parker and
John Smith to join together in the work necessitated by the Lord Protector's funeral, and to share the profits equally (Corporation of London Records Office; *London Citizens in 1651*, ed. Whitebrook, 23).
The Court of Common Council was an administrative court of the
municipal corporation of the City of London; the City was an important force in national politics at this time: see Valerie Pearl, *London*

and the Outbreak of the Puritan Revolution: City Government and National Politics, 1625–43 (Oxford: Oxford University Press, 1961); Robert Ashton, *The City and the Court 1603–1643* (Cambridge: Cambridge University Press, 1979); Lindley, *Popular Politics and Religion*. *Mr Smith* was perhaps the John Smith who worked with John Allen on Cromwell's funeral; however, *London Citizens in 1651* lists an Anthony mary a Smith as a member of the Company of Stainers along with Withy, Parker, and Allen. *Mr Radcliffe* was perhaps Hugh Ratcliffe, one of those involved in the second Root and Branch Petition, in December 1641, and a signatory of the Presbyterian petitions of 1645–46 (Lindley, *Popular Politics and Religion*, 139, 144). *Captain Palmer* was probably, given what Trapnel has just said, a sea captain, though I have been unable to trace him. It is possible, however, that he was Thomas Palmer (fl. 1644–66), who probably served as an officer in the army and then as chaplain to Skippon's regiment. He was vicar of St Lawrence Pountney from 1644–66, when he was made rector of Aston-on-Trent, Derbyshire. He was a Fifth Monarchist by 1654, and travelled and worked for the movement in the 1650s, especially in Nottingham and London. For *Mr Knollys*, see note 21.

42 *seal:* token of a covenant or promise.

43 *twelfth month . . . April:* i.e., February to April 1653.

44 *Mr Wythe:* perhaps the Mr Withy with whom John Allen (see note 41) worked; a member of the Company of Painter Stainers.

45 *Book of the Creature:* the Bible; "creature" is an obsolete form of "creator."

46 *Familistical ranting tenents: tenents* is an obsolete form of "tenets." Familists (members of the Family of Love) believed that heaven and hell are in the world among us; they held property in common, and believed that the spirit of God dwelt within each believer. Accusations of "ranting" were frequently levelled at any group or individual whose views the speaker/writer wanted to identify as "extreme" and ungodly, in order to distance themselves from them (Edward Thompson, "On the Rant," in *Reviving the English Revolution*, 153–60). Trapnel had been briefly involved with the Familists in 1652 (*Biographical Dictionary of British Radicals*, 3: 250), but is here distinguishing her own beliefs from theirs.

47 *Gath and Ashkelon:* two of the five chief Philistine cities. In 2 Samuel 1.20, David, lamenting the deaths of Saul and his son Jonathan, urges that the news of this should not be told in Gath or Ashkelon, "lest the daughters of the Philistines rejoice." They are thus places expected to be unsympathetic to the words of God's people.

48 *the calling in of the Jews:* Fifth Monarchists were awaiting the fulfilment of the biblical prophecies concerning the conversion and restoration

of the Jews, as this would be an indication that the millennium was near. See Cary, *A New and More Exact Mappe*, 139-60; John Tillinghast, *Generation-work* (London, 1655), 32-48; Capp, *Fifth Monarchy Men*, 190-91.

49 *the dissolution of the Parliament:* Cromwell expelled the Rump of the Long Parliament in April 1653, owing to their failure to introduce sufficiently innovative and radical reform. They were succeeded by the Barebones Parliament; see note 54.

50 *M.G. Harrison:* Major-General Thomas Harrison, who instigated the idea of the Nominated Assembly (Barebones Parliament); he sat in the Barebones Parliament, and was dismissed from the army in December 1653 for opposing the Protectorate. He was one of the most prominent Fifth Monarchists, greatly influenced by Simpson and Feake, but not himself a leader of the movement.

51 *Mr Speaker:* William Lenthall (1591-1662), a lawyer, was the Speaker of the House of Commons from 1640 (at the opening of the Long Parliament) until the dissolution of the Rump Parliament in April 1653.

52 *the minister of Hillingdon, Mr Taverner:* Philip Taverner was vicar of West Drayton, Buckinghamshire, and later rector of Hillingdon in Middlesex. Calamy called him "a grave, peaceable divine, of unblameable life" (Edmund Calamy, *The Nonconformist's Memorial*, 3 vols, [London: J. Cundee, 1802-3], 2: 458).

53 *linon draper·* trader dealing in linens, calicos, etc.

54 *this new representative:* the assembly that replaced the Rump Parliament, known as the Nominated Assembly or the Barebones Parliament, was summoned by Cromwell and composed of 140 men selected by the Army leaders: see Austin Woolrych, "The Calling of Barebone's Parliament," *English Historical Review* 80 (1965): 492-513; and Woolrych, *Commonwealth to Protectorate*, chap. 4 passim. The assembly met for the first time on 4 July 1653. Amongst the radical sectaries, there was a high degree of optimism about the potential of this parliament, as it was devised specifically as a parliament of the godly, or an "assembly of saints." However, rifts soon appeared between the more radical and conservative members, the latter began to gain ground, and finally, barely six months after its inauguration, this experiment in radical rule came to an end: on 12 December 1653, the conservative group, exploiting the radicals' absence at a prayer meeting, voted to invest all power in Cromwell as Lord Protector. Consequently, radicals such as Trapnel wrote bitterly of the betrayal of their hopes represented by this series of events. See Woolrych, "Calling of Barebone's Parliament" and *Comonwealth to Protectorate*; for discussions of the demise of the Rump Parliament, see Blair Worden, "The Bill for a New Representative," *English Historical Review* 86 (1971):

473–96; Worden, *The Rump Parliament 1648–1653* (London: Cambridge University Press, 1974).

55 *Colonel Bingham:* John Bingham (a moderate) sat in the Barebones Parliament, as well as in the parliaments of 1645–53, 1654, 1656 and 1659.

56 *Mr Barrett:* George Barrett was a Fifth Monarchist and Particular Baptist, and an assistant to Henry Jessey in 1653.

57 *linsey-woolsey party:* linsey-woolsey was originally a cloth woven from linen and wool, but also came to be used adjectivally, as here, to describe something that was a strange medley, nonsense, or in confusion. Trapnel is here probably making reference to the "moderate" group in Parliament.

58 *tabernacle work . . . temple work:* in Old Testament history, the tabernacle was superseded by the temple as the repository of the Ark of the Covenant and other sacred articles. Trapnel is here figuratively referring to the execution of God's work by Parliament and the failure of certain parliamentary factions to do so.

59 *the passing bell:* the bell rung immediately after a death; thus, here Trapnel is marking the passing of this party.

60 *the chairman, Mr Rous:* Francis Rous was Speaker for the Barebones Parliament, a moderate and a Presbyterian, who had sat in every parliament since 1626.

61 *tower:* a vision concerning the threat to "the rule of the saints." In the Bible, whiteness is associated with redemption; see Daniel 12.10; Revelation 3.4, 5; 4.4; 7.9; 19.8, 14. God is alluded to as a tower (with the idea of protection); see Psalm 61.3; Proverbs 18.10.

62 *a Babel:* see Genesis 11. The children of men built the city of Babel with a tower "whose top may reach to heaven." God took this as a sign of over-reaching human ambition and, as punishment, "confounded their language" so that they no longer all spoke the same language and could therefore not all understand each other any longer. A major topic in the seventeenth century: see Umberto Eco, *The Search for the Perfect Language,* trans. J. Feutress (Oxford: Blackwell, 1995).

63 *many oaks:* in Isaiah 2.13, Amos 2.9, and Zechariah 11.2, oaks signify loftiness, strength or pride that will be, or has been, humbled by God.

64 *Two nights before the Protector was established:* Cromwell was voted Lord Protector on 12 December 1653, and installed in this position on 15 December. Trapnel is thus probably referring here to 13 December.

65 *children . . . light shining around about them:* see Luke 16.8, John 12.36, Ephesians 5.8, and 1 Thessalonians 5.5 for references to "children of light," indicating true followers of God.

66 *a great company of cattle:* visions of cattle figure most famously in Pharaoh's dream in Genesis 41.

67 *the sepulchre was open:* on the third day after Christ's crucifixion, Mary
   Magdalene and Mary, James's mother, visited the sepulchre in which
   his body had been lain, to find it open and Christ departed. Christ
   then appeared to them as they went to tell the disciples of his absence. See Matthew 28; Mark 16; Luke 24; John 20.

68 *of Jesus ... resurrection:* these words were added in BL.

69 *Babylonians:* for the early Protestants, Babylon signified luxury, worldli-
   ness and ungodliness: "Babylon is fallen, is fallen, that great city, because she made all nations drink of the wine of the wrath of her forni-
   cation" (Revelation 14.8). See Revelation 16, 17, and 18 for other references to Babylon as the mystical city of the apocalypse.

70 —: such lines, included in the text either at the end or in the middle
   of paragraphs, indicate a break in the text: a missing word or, more
   often, passage which the relator was unable to take down.

71 *are my people jeered . .. my throne?:* a reference to the widespread hos-
   tility which met the extemporary prayer, testimony and prophesying
   characteristic of many of the radical sects.

72 *profession:* i.e., the profession of particular beliefs; sectarian writers frequently refer to their fellow sectaries as "professors."

73 *When Babylon ...:* on Babylon, see note 69. This verse section is set
   out in quatrains in BL. This is also the case for the following verse
   sections: "Oh, sing for Sion songs my soul" (p. 24); "O merchants! oh
   turn to the Lord" (p. 30); "Oh, it is that light that burneth bright" (p.
   41); "For human arts and sciences" (p. 46); "O that they may say
   unto death" (p. 49); and "Blessed be thy name oh thou Lord" (p. 74).
   For notes on less consistent differences between CUL and BL, see
   notes 154 and 202.

74 *the great:* "those great" in BL.

75 *cast them:* "them cast" in BL.

76 *they a while:* "a while they" in BL.

77 *you then do:* "then you do" in BL.

78 *What will become then of your pay:* soldiers' pay was a persistently contentious issue. Initially, after the founding of the New Model Army in
   April 1645, payment was maintained much more regularly than previously, but by 1647 it was seriously in arrears: "By February 1647 the
   soldiers were owed some £2,800,800 — the infantry being due eigh-
   teen weeks' arrears, the cavalry forty-three" (Charles Carlton, *Going
   to the Wars: The Experience of the English Civil Wars, 1638–1651* [Lon-
   don: BCA/Routledge, 1992], 317). In May 1647, Parliament proposed
   disbanding the army without settling these arrears; this contributed to
   the chain of events that led to the army's march on London in August
   1647 (see note 23). Pay arrears were still an issue in the early 1650s:
   one of the acts passed by the Barebones Parliament "provided for the

disposal of vast areas of Irish land to satisfy the 'Adventurers' who had advanced money on this security and to meet the arrears of pay of the army in Ireland" (Woolrych, _Commonwealth to Protectorate_, 304).

79 _sergeants that were honest men/Oh how are you fallen:_ initially the New Model Army seemed to sectaries as if it were to be an agent of radical change in the country. Sectarian expectations of the army were at their height during the invasion of Scotland in 1650, when the soldiers and junior officers of the Commonwealth army published the Declaration of Musselburgh. In this they claimed to be fighting for " 'the destruction of Antichrist and the advancement of the Kingdom of Jesus Christ.' They justified the execution of Charles as one of the ten horns of the beast (Rev. xvii), and declared they had 'proclaimed Jesus Christ, the King of Saints, to be our King by profession' " (Capp, _Fifth Monarchy Men_, 54). Cromwell's dismissal of the Rump in April 1653 had been effected with a troop of soldiers. The links between the army and the Fifth-Monarchy movement were strong: many Fifth Monarchists were recruited from the army: "some thirty-four Fifth Monarchists appear to have been officers, and at least fifty-six are identifiable as common soldiers. The true total of the latter was probably far higher" (ibid., 80). Early in January 1653, "soldiers and 'army preaching men' at Allhallows called for a new Parliament, but were silenced by army and government authorities" (ibid., 61). However, by 1654, sectaries felt betrayed by the army as a whole, as well as by Cromwell: the dissolution of the Barebones Parliament reinvested power in the army, as the officers had produced a new constitution, the Instrument of Government, under which Cromwell was given the position of Lord Protector. It was, however, principally the army grandees against whom the Fifth Monarchists inveighed; Trapnel, for example, still holds out hope that the rank and file will remain true to their earlier radical record. Hill writes of the power of this version of events within sectarian (particularly millenarian) politics: "The myth was that of the people's army, which had pledged itself never to disband or divide until its democratic objectives were obtained, treacherously overcome by Machiavellian generals who regarded it as a mere professional military machine which they used to further their own selfish aims and ambitions. And in betraying the people the generals had also betrayed God" (Hill, _The World Turned Upside Down_, 70).

80 _shall thus:_ "thus shall" in BL.

81 _thy servant that is now upon the throne:_ i.e., Cromwell. "is now" appears as "now is" in BL.

82 _Let them not ... Mordecai:_ see Esther 3–7. Mordecai, leader of the exiled Jewish community in Persia in the fourth century B.C., refused to bow to the treacherous anti-Jewish official, Haman, who tried to

get the Jews destroyed by slandering them at court. Haman is finally exposed (by Esther) and hanged on the gallows that he had had built for the execution of Mordecai. Mordecai subsequently becomes "prime minister." The "voice of Mordecai" is thus the voice of true loyalty and honesty (he had previously shown loyalty to the Persian king by disclosing a plot against his life), whilst "the voice of Haman," though apparently loyal, was actually treacherous, both to the Jews and to the king, since the destruction of the loyal Mordecai would not have been in the king's interests.

83 *Jacob's trouble ... travel:* Trapnel is here using "Jacob" as a name for the people of Israel, as was often the case in the Old Testament; the "trouble" would then refer to Israel's difficult history (such as in the Babylonian exile), and by extension to the Fifth-Monarchist struggle to prepare for the coming of King Jesus. The suggestion is that this had seemed imminent ("they had looked for a birth") but now seemed further away ("it is yet in travel"), owing to Cromwell's betrayal of the cause. "travel" = travail, labour.

84 *bowels:* as Cruden notes, bowels were "often used in Scripture for the seat of pity or kindness" (Alexander Cruden, *Cruden's Complete Concordance to the Bible*, rev. ed. [Cambridge: Lutterworth Press, 1977], 54). See, for example, Isaiah 63.15; Philippians 2.1; John 3.17.

85 *linsey-woolsey garments:* see note 57.

86 *Assyrian ... rod to Israel:* Assyria took Israel captive; see 2 Kings 17–19.

87 *a measuring time:* Trapnel's use of "measuring" here has the sense of "testing." See Ezekiel 40 and 41, Zechariah 2.1, and Revelation 11.1, 21.15 for the measuring of the holy city, the temple, and the New Jerusalem.

88 *Oh but ... in the valley:* Ezekiel has a vision of dry bones which, when he prophesies to them as God commands, are given flesh and breath by God. See Ezekiel 37.

89 *nations into this nation:* in the Bible, God's judgement is often exacted through the intervention of other nations: "The concept of an instrument of divine judgment — a nation chosen by God to bring on his own people and on others the disaster which is interpreted as the outcome of their failure — is one which Isaiah and others of the prophets employ with some frequency" (Charles M. Laymon, ed., *The Interpreter's One-Volume Commentary on the Bible* [London and Glasgow: Collins, 1971, repr. 1972], 339). More specifically, in Zechariah 14 the Day of Judgement is envisaged as "the nations of the world engaging in a final catastrophic battle against Jerusalem" (ibid., 336). Trapnel is suggesting that God would exact judgement on England were it not for the presence of the saints there.

90 *shall run:* "run shall" in BL.

91   *will thine:* "thine will" in BL.
92   *Grenado pieces:* grenades.
93   *their wide:* "wide their" in BL.
94   *soon shall:* "shall soon" in BL.
95   *the remnant:* a small number (originally of Jews) who survive persecution and in whom future hope is vested. See Isaiah 10.20–23.
96   *to Scotland . . . to Holland also:* see notes 31 and 39.
97   *stroke:* "strokes" in BL.
98   *landships:* a wagon or other vehicle serving the same purpose on land as a ship on the sea.
99   *to themselves:* "to" omitted in BL.
100 *I will not be your king:* Cromwell regularly considered the idea of becoming king, and the idea had been put forward by Lambert in December 1653; like Gideon, however (see note 33), Cromwell rejected it, though the proposition resurfaced regularly before he was formally offered it (and again rejected it) in 1657; see Hill, *God's Englishman*, 173–99; Sharpe, "An Image Doting Rabble." Trapnel, however, accuses him of being king in all but name (see note 224).
101 *canded:* obsolete form of "candied."
102 *Mount Sion:* hill on the south-west side of Jerusalem; by extension, Jerusalem itself.
103 *Mordecai . . . hang without:* see note 82. Mordecai "called in," while Haman hangs without, is a reference to Mordecai's promotion following the execution of Haman. The story illustrates the point that those who think their position is assured will be cast out, and vice versa.
104 *fain:* glad, well-pleased.
105 *Adam's state before:* i.e., before the Fall; see Genesis 3.
106 *O prophets all:* prophecy had a much broader meaning in the seventeenth century than it does today: "prophecy was any utterance produced by God through human agency" (Purkiss, "Producing the Voice, Consuming the Body," 139). Mary Cary, another Fifth-Monarchist prophet, extended the definition still further: "all might prophesy, that is (in the lowest sense) be able to speak to edification, exhortation and comfort" (Cary, *A New and More Exact Mappe*, 237). Cary is here referring to Paul's definition of prophecy in 1 Corinthians 14.3. For Trapnel to refer to the "saints" as "prophets all," therefore, was no more than a sectarian orthodoxy. For a fuller discussion of the meanings of prophecy in the seventeenth century, see the Introduction, pp. xiii–xv.
107 *O, Canaan, saints . . . due time:* these four lines were added in BL.
108 *Joshuas . . . Calebs:* Joshua and Caleb were the only two of the leaders of the twelve tribes of Israel not to question God's commandments concerning the occupation of Canaan, the homeland prom-

ised to the exiled Israelites; consequently, God punished the other ten by destroying them, allowing only their children to enter into the promised land, and rewarding the loyalty of Joshua and Caleb: "Your carcases shall fall in this wilderness; and all that numbered of you, according to your whole number from twenty years old and upward, which have murmured against me, Doubtless ye shall not come into the land, concerning which I sware to make you dwell therein, save Caleb the son of Jephunneh, and Joshua the son of Nun" (Numbers 14.29–30). Joshua and Caleb thus signify those of God's chosen people who do not backslide, but keep faith with God's commands.

109 *Canaan's land*: the promised land, "the land of milk and honey" (Numbers 13.27); see note 108.

110 *smothers*: smoke, or smouldering fires.

111 *notioners*: a variant form of "notionists": those whom the speaker/ writer deems to hold extravagant and wrong-headed religious opinions.

112 *Hallelujahs*: "Hallelujah" in BL.

113 *with thee upon the mount*: scriptural prophets typically communed with God on mountains (e.g., Moses on Mount Sinai); Jesus is associated with the Mount of Olives and, as the reference here is to the Transfiguration (Matthew 17.1–9), with Mount Tabor.

114 *provision for a poor man . . .*: probably a reference to Cromwell, who grew up "conscious of the fact that he was a poor relation"; his father had £300 a year (Hill, *God's Englishman*, 38).

115 *a Jacob, a dew, a lion*: "And the remnant of Jacob shall be in the midst of many people as a dew from the Lord, as the showers upon the grass, that tarrieth not for man, nor waiteth for the sons of men. And the remnant of Jacob shall be among the Gentiles in the midst of many people as a lion among the beasts of the forest, as a young lion among the flocks of sheep; who, if he go through, both treadeth down, and teareth in pieces, and none can deliver" (Micah 5.7–8). For "remnant," see note 95.

116 *your callings, your offices*: a calling was an occupation, trade or business (as well as a vocation); offices were general duties towards others, moral obligations, sometimes attaching to one's station, position or employment. "&c" was added after these words in BL.

117 *sour leaven*: in 1 Corinthians 5.6–8, Paul suggests that the lax attitudes of spokesmen for the church are like leaven, infecting the entire congregation: "In Paul's thought the yeast or other leavening organism is associated with the process of putrefaction and corruption" (Laymon, *One-Volume Commentary*, 800). Thus Trapnel is here suggesting that ungodly leaders are corrupting God's people.

118 line of omission added here in BL.

119 *a*: added in BL.

120   *Ezekiels . . . river Chebar:* Ezekiel received a number of visions from
      God by the river of Chebar; see Ezekiel 1.1–3; 3.15, 23; 10.15, 20.
121   line of omission added here in BL.
122   *free grace for all:* free grace is "the undeserved gift of God's love
      which can never be known or experienced save by the surrender of
      all trust in human skills and ability and the surrender to Jesus as
      Lord" (Laymon, *One-Volume Commentary*, 934); "the free and un-
      merited favour of God as manifested in the salvation of sinners and
      the bestowing of blessings" (OED). For Trapnel's most extended dis-
      cussion of free grace, see her work *A Legacy for Saints* (London,
      1654). The apparently contradictory beliefs manifested in Trapnel's
      (and much other) writing, that a) free grace is "for all," and b) only
      a predestined "elect" will be saved, constitute what von Rohr iden-
      tifies as a fundamental duality within Puritan thought; the paradox
      is summarised usefully in a quotation he includes from Jenison's
      Christ's Death and Love (1642): "Here then is the mystery: Though
      God invite all, and promise life to all upon the condition of faith,
      . . . yet the fruit of Christ's death doth actually belong . . . to the
      Elect only" (quoted in John von Rohr, *The Covenant of Grace in
      Puritan Thought* [Atlanta: Scholars Press, 1986], 129). Von Rohr's
      book offers an exhaustive and illuminating exploration of this duality
      in relation to seventeenth-century Puritan writing.
123   *mercy seat:* "the golden covering of the ark of the covenant in which
      the tables of the law were deposited" (Cruden, *Complete Concor-
      dance*, 429).
124   *love them:* "them love" in BL.
125   *God-man:* Christ: God in his human incarnation.
126   *he . . . lustre:* perhaps an echo of Ambrose's *Splendor Paternae Gloriae;*
      I am grateful to Leslie S. B. MacCoull for this suggestion.
127   *King Jesus:* Fifth Monarchists were awaiting and preparing for the
      (imminent) arrival of Jesus, when he would assume his place as
      "king" of the fifth monarchy.
128   *written:* "writers" in CUL; BL version given here as more likely.
129   *Oh draw near:* "Oh draw, draw near" in BL.
130   *And say unto the living Lord:* "Oh say unto the loving Lord" in BL.
131   *up:* word added in BL.
132   *then they:* "they then" in BL.
133   *and after:* "and then after" in BL.
134   *language of Canaan . . . language of Ashdod:* Canaan was the land
      promised by God to Abraham for the Israelites; Ashdod was the city
      to which the Philistines took the ark of God when they stole it from
      the Israelites. The city was destroyed by God as punishment. See 1
      Samuel 5.

135 *university learning and the national clergy:* Fifth Monarchists, like all
sectaries, were generally dismissive, even contemptuous, of university
education: "They stressed that ministers were made by God, not by
education, and denied that university-trained men were true ministers unless also called by a congregation" (Capp, *Fifth Monarchy
Men*, 188). This was largely because the universities' main function
was to train the "national clergy" — the ministers of the Church of
England — to whose privileges and doctrines the sects were opposed.
Both universities and clergy were seen as cornerstones of the system
which they were striving to change; and both were funded, directly
or indirectly, by tithes — a much-resented tax and one of the main
targets of all the radical sects, but which were, in the end, never
abolished. See note 138.

136 *it then:* "then it" in BL.

137 *seers:* prophets; see note 106.

138 *maintenance:* the clergy of the Church of England were maintained
by tithes, a compulsory tax which weighed heavily on poorer people.
Sectaries argued that tithes should be abolished and the clergy maintained by voluntary contributions by their parishioners; this, of
course, would have made them much more accountable to their congregations. Moreover, it would have spelt the end of the established
church: "An established church stood or fell with tithes. Election
and payment of ministers by congregations would mean the end of
any nationally controlled and disciplined church. It would make anything but complete religious toleration virtually impossible" (Hill,
Century of Revolution, 140). Opposition to tithes was consistent
across the different sects and throughout the years of the Civil War,
Commonwealth, and Protectorate: even in 1659, the year before
Charles II was restored to the throne, Quaker women presented to
Parliament a petition against tithes of 7,000 women's signatures, "a
major feat of political organization" (Patricia Crawford, "The Challenges to Patriarchalism: How did the Revolution Affect Women?,"
in *Revolution and Restoration: England in the 1650s*, ed. John Morrill
[London: Collins and Brown, 1992], 112–28, here 126).

139 *trumpeters with a full sound ... battle:* In 1 Corinthians 14, Paul emphasises the importance of clarity in prophesying; in the verse following the one Trapnel is paraphrasing here, he wrote, "except ye
utter by the tongue words easy to be understood, how shall it be
known what is spoken? for ye shall speak into the air" (1 Corinthians 14.9).

140 *carnal studies:* worldly knowledge.

141 *timbrels:* a timbrel was a kind of tambourine, played at times of celebration and thanksgiving. See, for example, 2 Samuel 6.5; Psalms

68.25, 150.4. It was the instrument of Miriam, the woman prophet, in Exodus 15.20–21.

142 *thy people are accounted by the world a people of much affections, but of little judgement:* sectaries were characterised by their opponents as governed only by their emotions ("affections") rather than by sound reason or judgement: "their affections are raised by figures, and earnestness and passionate representations; by the circumstances of the voice, and gesture, and motion ... we ought to feed our people with wholsome food, and not with trash, and poyson, though they long never so much for them" (Joseph Glanvill, *An Essay Concerning Preaching* [London, 1677], 55–56, 58).

143 *sun:* the coming of Christ is compared with the rising of the sun in Malachi 4.2: "But unto you that fear my name shall the Sun of righteousness arise with healing in his wings; and ye shall go forth, and grow up as calves of the stall." Earlier cited in play on words (p. 32); and alluded to again below (pp. 49, 51, 62, 64, and 77).

144 *Pale-faced death:* death is not "pale-faced" in the Bible, though in Revelation 6.8, Death rides on a "pale horse."

145 *rest:* in Hebrews 4.1–11, "rest" (in the sense of "peace of spirit" or "the kingdom of heaven") is promised "for we which have believed."

146 *breath:* life dependent upon God; see Genesis 2.7; Job 12.10, 33.4; Ezekiel 37.5; Daniel 5.23; Acts 17.25.

147 *created pieces:* creatures.

148 *first day:* Sunday; the day of rest.

149 *to poor women:* when Christ rose from the dead, he appeared first to women; see note 67.

150 *Rabboni:* "my master'; see John 20.16.

151 *Let there be no more ... into her earth:* the implication here is of an opposition between a carnal voice and a godly voice.

152 *thou sentest down a ladder to the earth:* Jacob dreamt of a ladder extending from heaven to earth, on which were "the angels of God ascending and descending" (Genesis 28.12). Here, however, the suggestion is that Christ is a ladder by means of which human beings might ascend to heaven; cf. Trapnel, *A Legacy for Saints*, 35.

153 *the human nature ... divine:* as in the so-called "Athanasian Creed": "Not by the conversion of the Godhead into flesh, but by the taking of the manhood into God." Thanks to Leslie S. B. MacCoull for this reference.

154 *Oh thou art rest ...:* set out in quatrains up to "thou bringst in" in BL.

155 *may:* "may" appears as "might" in BL.

156 *surplices and tippets:* articles of clergymen's clothing: a surplice is a white linen vestment worn over the cassock, a tippet an ecclesiastical scarf.

157 *university language, their headpiece language:* on sectarian attitudes to university learning, see note 135. "Headpiece" means head, as seat of the intellect, or brain (OED). The implication is that their university education means that the clergy rely on their learning, their heads, rather than the scriptures ("the voice of the New Covenant teaching"), for their preaching, in order to baffle and deceive people about God's true message.

158 *New Covenant teaching:* teaching of or about Christ. The New Covenant was the new and better replacement of the old Mosaic covenant promised by the prophet Jeremiah (Jeremiah 31.31-34), one that would go to the heart rather than consisting in outward symbols and institutions. Jesus interprets his coming as the coming of the New Covenant (1 Corinthians 11.25; Matthew 26.28).

159 *beast:* i.e., Satan, as in Revelation.

160 *men shall not always be content . . . thy spirit:* another instance of the opposition between "carnal," or worldly, and godly understanding.

161 *palaces:* Cromwell took the palaces of Whitehall and Hampton Court as his residences when he became Lord Protector.

162 *this was not Gideon of old:* see note 33.

163 *his chief council:* the Council of State. According to Woolrych's table (Woolrych, *Commonwealth to Protectorate,* 403-33), approximately 80 percent of the first Protectorial Council of State were Justices of the Peace. They appointed a committee on 3 January 1654 "to regulate the justices of the peace throughout the country, but the only men among their former opponents in the House to be struck off the commission of the peace were Harrison, Danvers, Bawden, and Carew" (ibid., 387).

164 *their fat, and fleeces:* their share of the material benefits of power and influence (the biblical passage refers to the Old Testament priest's due). This sense of "fat" survives in the phrase "the fat of the land'; "fleece" had the sense "a share of booty" (OED).

165 *the pastors of churches . . . own thee:* Trapnel is here referring to the recognition and support of Cromwell by some of the clergy.

166 *Jezebels:* Jezebel was the proud and ruthless wife of King Ahab, king of Israel; used allusively of a wicked, impudent or abandoned woman, or for a woman who paints her face (see 1 Kings 26.31; 19; 2 Kings 9; and cf. Revelation 2.20).

167 *locks:* hair.

168 *Eli of old:* Eli was a high priest and judge, chosen by God (1 Samuel 2.28). He was punished by God (1 Samuel 4) for the sins of his sons, "because his sons made themselves vile, and he restrained them not" (1 Samuel 3.13).

169 *he is a sealed one:* "to seal" has a specific meaning in a New Testa-

ment context: "to designate, set apart, assign to another person or bind together, by an inviolable token or pledge" (OED). "And grieve not the Holy Spirit, whereby ye are sealed unto the day of redemption" (Ephesians 4.30). "A sealed one," then, is one to whom God has made an irrevocable promise. See also John 6.27; Ephesians 1.13; Revelation 7.

170   *bands:* shackles or fetters.

171   *Delilahs:* Delilah persuaded Samson to reveal to her the secret of his strength (which was in his uncut hair), and then betrayed him to the Philistines. See Judges 16.

172   *Abraham was for five righteous ones:* God agreed to spare the city of Sodom, which he was planning to destroy because of its wickedness, if fifty righteous people were found there. Abraham bargained with him: "Peradventure there shall lack five of the fifty righteous: wilt thou destroy all the city for lack of five? And he said, If I find there forty and five, I will not destroy it" (Genesis 18.28).

173   *Absalom:* see note 29.

174   *Gideon, in Scotland:* see notes 31, 34.

175   *Jacob:* see note 83. "Jacob" here again refers to the people of Israel as a whole. Gideon was the underdog, cowed by the Midianite enemy, but God used him to deliver Israel against impossible odds. See Judges 6, 7.

176   *Ninevites' king:* when Jonah called on the people of Nineveh to repent, their king decreed that all should take heed of his message, urging that all should "turn every one from his evil way, and from the violence that is in their hands" (Jonah 3.7). The attentive and penitent Ninevite king is a model of how people should respond to the admonitions of a prophet.

177   *a dish of herbs . . . stalled ox:* "Better is a dinner of herbs where love is, than a stalled ox and hatred therewith" (Proverbs 15.17).

178   *strength may be in thy locks:* see note 171.

179   *thorough:* through.

180   *Queen-mother . . . as a flood:* "And the serpent cast out of his mouth water as a flood after the woman, that he might cause her to be carried away of the flood. And the earth helped the woman; and the earth opened her mouth, and swallowed up the flood which the dragon cast out of his mouth" (Revelation 12.15–16); "the woman symbolizes the church, the true Israel . . . the scene symbolizes the protection of the church, providentially saved from the onslaughts of Satan" (Laymon, *One-Volume Commentary*, 960).

181   *wise Agar:* i.e., Hagar. Hagar was Abraham and Sarah's servant. When Sarah did not conceive, she sent Hagar to Abraham, who, as a result of their encounter, had a son, Ishmael. Subsequently Sarah

too had a son, Isaac, who took precedence over Ishmael because he was born to a free woman, whilst Ishmael's mother was a bond-woman. Hagar is "wise," then, because she accepted the harsh treatment she received at Sarah's hands and was rewarded by God for it. See Genesis 16; 21; for an allegorical reading of the story, see Galatians 4.24.

182 *his sick-bed:* Cromwell suffered from recurrent attacks of fever, perhaps a type of malaria, after his campaign in Ireland in 1649–50; he had an intense and prolonged attack in Scotland in the first half of 1651. These attacks continued until his death in 1658.

183 *to Worcester he did come:* at the Battle of Worcester, on 3 September 1651, a year to the day after the Battle of Dunbar, the Commonwealth armies, led by Cromwell, routed an invading Scottish army, led by the future Charles II. The victory at Worcester, at which point the army was at its most united, brought the civil wars to an end and elevated Cromwell to the high point of his standing with the radicals. As the Fifth Monarchist Hugh Peter put it, "When your wives and children shall ask you where you have been, and what news: say you have been in Worcester, where England's sorrows began, where they were happily ended" (Peter, quoted in Carlton, *Going to the Wars*, 338).

184 *into the city he must come:* after the Battle of Worcester, Cromwell ceased to be personally involved in military action, but became a full-time politician and statesman resident in the capital (Peter Gaunt, *Oliver Cromwell* [Oxford: Blackwell, 1996], 133–34). Cromwell himself spoke of his disappointment on going to London, to which Trapnel also refers here; see Gaunt, *Oliver Cromwell*, 135–37.

185 *redshanks:* a derogatory name for the Celtic inhabitants of the Scottish Highlands or Ireland.

186 *Jeremiah:* the people of Jerusalem rejected Jeremiah and his prophecies: "Then said they, Come, and let us devise devices against Jeremiah; for the law shall not perish from the priest, nor counsel from the wise, nor the word from the prophet: come, and let us smite him with the tongue, and let us not give heed to any of his words" (Jeremiah 18.18).

187 *this palace:* i.e., the Palace of Whitehall, where Trapnel had fallen into the trance. For the phraseology, cf. Psalm 122.7.

188 *sergeants:* see note 79.

189 *foolish virgins:* the parable of the ten virgins is told in Matthew 25.1–13. The five wise virgins had oil in their lamps ready for the arrival of the bridegroom, and were able to go out and meet him, whilst the five foolish virgins, who had no oil, were unable to, and were subsequently turned away by him for being unprepared. The parable con-

cludes, "Watch therefore, for ye know neither the day nor the hour wherein the Son of man cometh." See, too, title of the dedicatory epistle to this text, p. 2.

190   *painted looks:* feigned or deceptive appearances. Perhaps also a reference to dissenting opposition to images; cf. "graven images," p. 69.

191   *flashily:* like a flash of light: brief, transient.

192   *spirits:* "spirit" in BL.

193   *the form without the power:* Paul warns against those "having a form of godliness, but denying the power thereof" (2 Timothy 3.5). This phrase is often used in sectarian writings to distinguish between the truly godly and those who have yet to find the truth or who only feign godliness.

194   *thy people ... the sun:* "try" here has the sense of "separate out from"; "in face of" means "in defiance of, in direct opposition to" (*OED*). Thus God's people, Trapnel suggests, will separate themselves out from the Ranters, because the latter are known to be in defiance of Christ. For more about the Ranters, see A. L. Morton, *The World of the Ranters: Religious Radicalism in the English Revolution* (London: Lawrence and Wishart, 1970); Hill, *The World Turned Upside Down*, 203–10; Nigel Smith, ed., *A Collection of Ranter Writings from the Seventeenth Century* (London: Junction Books, 1983); Thompson, "On the Rant."

195   *thine indeed are for Christ within them:* Fifth Monarchists believed that Christ dwelt within each believer.

196   *the New Jerusalem:* following the day of judgement, the New Jerusalem would be instigated; it was prophesied in Isaiah 65.17–25, and in Revelation : "And I John saw the holy city, new Jerusalem, coming down from God out of heaven, prepared as a bride adorned for her husband" (Revelation 21.2). Here there will be "no more death, neither sorrow, nor crying, neither shall there be any more pain: for the former things are passed away" (Revelation 21.4). Here, under the rule of King Jesus, is the Fifth Monarchy for which Trapnel and her fellow believers are preparing. See Cary, *A New and More Exact Mappe*.

197   *Joshua:* see note 108.

198   *legal:* i.e., pertaining to the Law, the Old Testament (as opposed to the Gospel or New Testament).

199   *offended in Baal:* Baal was the Canaanite sun-god, the chief agent in the production of plenteous crops. The Israelites periodically lapsed from the worship of God to the worship of Baal. The phrase "offended in Baal" comes from Hosea 13.1.

200   *Demas:* Demas, a Gentile, is mentioned by Paul as one of his fellow workers who were with him during his imprisonment, presumably in

Rome or Ephesus. Tradition has it that the relationship between Demas and Paul ended in unresolved rupture: "For Demas hath forsaken me, having loved this present world, and is departed unto Thessalonica" (2 Timothy 4.10). This is usually taken to suggest Demas's apostasy from Christianity. See Freedman, *Anchor Bible Dictionary*, 2: 134–35.

201   *the sun discovers all things:* see note 143.

202   *He that did . . .:* set out in quatrains up to ". . . thou wouldst dry up" in BL.

203   *he would open . . . he would tear:* for John's vision of the book sealed with seven seals, and the opening thereof, see Revelation 5.

204   *Gog and Magog:* in Revelation 20.8, Gog and Magog represent the nations of the earth deceived by Satan. See too Ezekiel 38 and 39. Hugh Peter, the radical Fifth-Monarchist army chaplain, wrote of the interest in prophecies such as this: "Some looking to the prophecies that concern *Gog* and *Magog:* some casting their eye upon the drying up of *Euphrates,* . . . and most men disputing the slaying of the two witnesses; as much conducing to Gods designe in bringing about . . . the fifth Monarchy" (Hugh Peter, quoted in Capp, *Fifth Monarchy Men,* 44).

205   *John . . . the great fall:* John writes of the fall of Babylon in Revelation 17–19.

206   *a book write sweet:* probably a reference to the book of Revelation, in particular Revelation 10.9–10.

207   *principal:* deputy or agent.

208   *confound their language:* see note 62.

209   *Jeroboams . . . Israel to sin:* Jeroboam encouraged the people of Israel to turn away from God and worship idols; see 1 Kings 12.26–33.

210   *restauration, and generation-work:* "restauration" refers to "the reinstatement of man in the divine favour or in a state of innocence" (*OED*). "Generation-work": Trapnel is doubtless alluding here to a book published the previous year, in 1653, by John Tillinghast, entitled *Generation-work.* Tillinghast argues that "Generation-work is that work, or those works, which the way or manner of God's dispensations in the age a saint lives in, calls him unto" (p. 5); it is "of all others the greatest works, and neglect herein the greatest sin" (p. 15). After a lengthy investigation of what characterises the present age, he concludes that:

> the work of the present generation, which saints are bound to attend to, and to be active in, lies principally in these things: the conversion of the Jews, propagation of the Gospel, in order to a greater harvest of Gentiles, joynting [sic]

saints (Christ['s] mystical body) into one. Pulling down of all high and lofty things, and persons, that oppose Christ. The establishment of justice and righteousness in the world, striving with God in a more especial manner for a greater degree of his spirit, more light and grace than saints in former generations have had; together with the exaltation of Christ as King, both in his churches and also over the world" (p. 48).

Tillinghast (1604-55) was a Fifth Monarchist and Independent minister, "the most learned of the Fifth Monarchists," and the only one capable of publishing a systematic analysis of the prophetic texts basic to the movement (*Biographical Dictionary of British Radicals*, 3: 241-42). He published two additional, and increasingly apocalyptic, parts to *Generation-work*, in 1654 and 1655, and the three parts were republished in one volume in 1655.

211   *many whose god is their belly:* i.e., those ruled by their carnal appetites.

212   *take turns in your galleries:* promenade in the galleries of your fine houses.

213   *Assyrian:* see note 86.

214   *Philistine without:* the external enemy. The Philistines were in early times the Israelites' most persistent opponents.

215   *council:* i.e., the Council of State; see note 8.

216   *Goliah:* Goliath.

217   *Scotland, Ireland:* the parliamentary army, under Cromwell, conducted campaigns in both Scotland and Ireland (see Gentles, *The New Model Army in England, Ireland and Scotland*); the Irish one is renowned as a particularly brutal one. It is not clear what Trapnel is wanting to communicate to the soldiers by means of this reference.

218   *the condition of Job:* Elihu reproaches Job's three friends for condemning Job without justification; see Job 32, especially verses 17-22.

219   *some poor creatures . . . head and members:* some sectaries, such as some Ranters, concluded that there was no difference between Christ and his believers, because Christ dwelt within them; Trapnel refutes this conclusion here. See Hill, *The World Turned Upside Down*, 204-8.

220   *they say . . . crucified Jesus:* Trapnel here is distinguishing herself from some of her audience with whose views she disagrees.

221   *Gath . . . Askelon:* see note 47.

222   *formerly their children . . . so it is now:* Trapnel is here using the fashionable practices of the aristocracy to refer metonymically to the vesting of power in the higher echelons of society once more. Fifth

Monarchists were commonly scathing of such practices: Hugh Peter, in his dedicatory epistle to Mary Cary's *The Little Horns Doom and Downfall* (London, 1651), praised Cary by distancing her from such worldly concerns: "in this dress you shall neither see naked Brests, black Patches, nor long Trains; but an heart breathing after the *coming of Christ*, and the *comfort of Saints*" (Cary, *Little Horns Doom and Downfall*, a2ʳ). Trapnel herself, earlier in *The Cry of a Stone*, has referred disparagingly to "you that are proud, ... / And mincingly do go, /With your black spots and powdered locks /Thinking to make a show (p. 31).

223   *How can they be fit to rule ... reprove their own families:* Cromwell's son, Richard, was known for his lack of devotion to God and an attachment to expensive living, which got him into debt. Similarly, Lucy Hutchinson wrote, "Cleypoole, who married his [i.e., Cromwell's] daughter, and his son Henry, were two debauch'd ungodly cavaliers" (Lucy Hutchinson, *Memoirs of the Life of Colonel Hutchinson* [London: Kegan, Paul, Trench, Trubner & Co., 1904], 351); see Sherwood, *The Court of Oliver Cromwell*.

224   *hadst not thou better ... rent from thee?:* Trapnel suggests it would have been better that Cromwell had died in battle rather than to have assumed the trappings of power in the way that he has, by becoming Lord Protector. On "palace," see note 161.

225   *and:* if, as long as.

226   *Daniels:* Daniel was noted for not succumbing to flattery, but, in spite of it, continuing to tell the truth. See Daniel 5.13–29.

227   *New Covenant sermon:* see note 158.

228   *thy very palace:* the palace of Whitehall, where Trapnel had fallen into her trance, was one of Cromwell's residences.

229   *wind:* God's workings are often compared with the wind; see e.g., Acts 2.2; in Amos 1.14, a palace is destroyed by a whirlwind.

230   *Sodom:* one of the Cities of the Plain destroyed by God for their sinfulness (Genesis 19.24–25).

231   *fourth great monarchy:* Fifth Monarchists believed that the world had thus far seen four great monarchies: the empires of Babylon, Assyria (or the Medes and the Persians), Greece, and Rome, the latter still oppressing Europe in the form of the Roman Catholic church and, by extension, the Anglican church. This is the "fourth monarchy," which would be destroyed at the Last Judgement to make way for the fifth and everlasting one: God's kingdom on earth, the establishing of the New Jerusalem, and the return of Christ as king.

232   *these beatings of thy spices:* see Exodus 30.34–36: spices were beaten, and put "before the testimony in the tabernacle of the congregation, where I will meet with thee: it shall be unto you most holy."

233 *the seal of God:* the "seal" in this context means "a token or symbol
     of a covenant" (OED).
234 *Sun:* "Son" in BL.
235 *the thine: sic* in BL; this is a correction of CUL's "thes thine."

BIBLIOGRAPHY

Primary Sources

Cary, Mary. *The Little Horns Doom and Downfall*. London, 1651.

——. *A New and More Exact Mappe or Description of New Jerusalems Glory*. London, 1651.

Channel, Elinor. *A Message from God (By a Dumb Woman)*. London, 1653.

Glanvill, Joseph. *An Essay Concerning Preaching*. London, 1677.

Tillinghast, John. *Generation-work: or A Brief and Seasonable Word, offered to the view and consideration of the Saints and People of God in this Generation, relating to the Work of the present Age, or Generation we live in*. London, 1653, 2nd ed. 1655.

Trapnel, Anna. *Strange and Wonderful Newes from White-hall*. London, 1654. Wing, Short Title Catalogue (hereafter STC) no. T2034.

——. *The Cry of a Stone*. London, 1654. Wing, STC no. T2031.

——. *A Legacy for Saints*. London, 1654. Wing, STC no. T2032.

——. *Anna Trapnel's Report and Plea*. London, 1654. Wing, STC no. T2033.

——. *A Voice for the King of Saints*. London, 1658. Wing, STC no. T2035.

——. 1000-page folio, title page missing, in Bodleian Library, Oxford; n.d.

Secondary Works

Apocrypha. Oxford: Oxford University Press, 1926.

Ashton, Robert. *The City and the Court 1603–1643*. Cambridge: Cambridge University Press, 1979.

Ballaster, Ros. *Seductive Forms: Women's Amatory Fiction from 1684 to 1740*. Oxford: Clarendon Press, 1992.

Barker, Francis. *The Tremulous Private Body*. London: Methuen, 1984.

Batsleer, Janet, Tony Davies, Rebecca O'Rourke and Chris Weedon. *Rewriting English: Cultural Politics of Gender and Class*. London: Methuen, 1985.

Beaven, Alfred B. *The Aldermen of the City of London*. 2 vols. London: Eden Fisher and Co., 1908–13.

Bell, Maureen, George Parfitt, and Simon Shepherd. *A Biographical Diction-*
ary of English Women Writers 1580-1720. London: Harvester Wheatsheaf, 1990.

Belsey, Catherine. *The Subject of Tragedy: Identity and Difference in Renais-*
sance Drama. London: Methuen, 1985.

———. *Desire: Love Stories in Western Culture*. Oxford: Blackwell, 1994.

Berg, Christina and Philippa Berry. "Spiritual Whoredom: An Essay on
Female Prophets in the Seventeenth Century." In *1642: Literature and*
Power in the Seventeenth Century, ed. Francis Barker et al., 37-54. Col-
chester, Essex: University of Essex Press, 1981.

Brockington, L. H. *A Critical Introduction to the Apocrypha*. London: Ger-
ald Duckworth and Co. Ltd., 1961.

Brown, Louise Fargo. *The Political Activities of the Baptists and Fifth Mon-*
archy Men in England during the Interregnum. Burt Franklin Research
and Resource Series 97. New York: Burt Franklin, 1911.

Burckhardt, Jacob. *The Civilization of the Renaissance in Italy*. trans.
S. G. C. Middlemore. London: George G. Harrap and Co. Ltd., 1929.

Burke, Seán. "Changing Conceptions of Authorship." In *Authorship: From*
Plato to the Postmodern, ed. Seán Burke, 5-11. Edinburgh: Edinburgh
University Press, 1995.

Burrage, Champlin. "Anna Trapnel's Prophecies." *English Historical Re-*
view 26 (1911): 526-35.

Calamy, Edmund. *The Nonconformist's Memorial*, 2nd ed., ed. Samuel Palmer. 3 vols. London: J. Cundee, 1802-3.

Caldwell, Patricia. *The Puritan Conversion Narrative: The Beginnings of*
American Expression. Cambridge: Cambridge University Press, 1983.

Capp, Bernard. *The Fifth Monarchy Men: A Study in Seventeenth-Century*
English Millenarianism. London: Faber and Faber, 1972.

———. "The Fifth Monarchists and Popular Millenarianism." In *Radical*
Religion in the English Revolution, ed. J. F. McGregor and B. Reay, 165-
89. Oxford: Oxford University Press, 1984.

———. *Cromwell's Navy: The Fleet and the English Revolution 1648-1660*. Oxford: Clarendon Press, 1989.

Carlton, Charles. *Going to the Wars: The Experience of the English Civil*
Wars, 1638-1651. London: BCA/Routledge, 1992.

Carr, Helen, ed. *From My Guy to Sci-Fi: Genre and Women's Writing in the*
Postmodern World. London: Pandora, 1989.

de Certeau, Michel. *The Practice of Everyday Life*, trans. Steven F. Rendall.
Berkeley, Los Angeles, London: University of California Press, 1984.

Chedgzoy, Kate. "Female Prophecy in the Seventeenth Century: The Instance of Anna Trapnel." In *Writing and the English Renaissance*, ed.
William Zunder and Suzanne Trill, 238-54. Harlow: Longman, 1996.

Clow, W. M., ed. *The Bible Reader's Encyclopaedia and Concordance*. rev.

ed. London and New York: Collins, 1962.

Coggins, R. J. and J. L Houlden, eds. *A Dictionary of Biblical Interpretation.* London: SCM Press, 1990.

Cohen, Alfred. "The Fifth Monarchy Mind: Mary Cary and the Origins of Totalitarianism." *Social Research* 31 (1964): 195–213.

Cohn, Norman. *The Pursuit of the Millennium: Revolutionary Millenarians and Mystical Anarchists of the Middle Ages,* 3rd ed. London: Pimlico, 1993.

Collinson, Patrick. *The Religion of Protestants: The Church in English Society 1559–1625.* Oxford: Clarendon Press, 1982.

Comay, Joan. *Who's Who in the Old Testament, together with the Apocrypha.* London: Weidenfeld and Nicolson, 1971.

Cook, Chris and John Wroughton. *English Historical Facts 1603–1688.* London: Macmillan, 1980.

Cope, Esther S., ed. *Prophetic Writings of Lady Eleanor Douglas. Women Writers in English 1350–1850.* New York and Oxford: Oxford University Press, 1995.

Crawford, Patricia. "The Challenges to Patriarchalism: How did the Revolution Affect Women?" In *Revolution and Restoration: England in the 1650s,* ed. John Morrill, 112–28. London: Collins and Brown, 1992.

———. *Women and Religion in England 1500–1720.* London and New York: Routledge, 1993.

Cressy, David. *Literacy and the Social Order: Reading and Writing in Tudor and Stuart England.* Cambridge: Cambridge University Press, 1980.

Cruden, Alexander. *Cruden's Complete Concordance to the Bible,* rev ed Cambridge, Butterworth Press, 1977.

CSPD: Public Record Office, *Calendar of State Papers: Domestic Series,* 1547–1704: 1653, 1654. London: HMSO, 1856–1972.

Dailey, Barbara Ritter. "The Visitation of Sarah Wight: Holy Carnival and the Revolution of the Saints in Civil War London." *Studies in Church History* 55 (1986): 438–55.

Darlington, Ida and James Howgego. *Printed Maps of London: Circa 1553–1850.* 2nd ed. London: Dawson, 1974.

Davies, Stevie. *Unbridled Spirits: Women of the English Revolution 1640–1660.* London: The Women's Press, 1998.

Delany, Paul. *British Autobiography in the Seventeenth Century.* London: Routledge and Kegan Paul, 1969.

DNB: Stephen, L., and S. Lee, eds. *Dictionary of National Biography.* 21 vols. and suppl. Oxford: Oxford University Press, 1921–22.

Dollimore. Jonathan. *Radical Tragedy: Religion, Ideology and Power in the Drama of Shakespeare and his Contemporaries.* 2nd ed. Hemel Hempstead: Harvester Wheatsheaf, 1989.

———. *Sexual Dissidence: Augustine to Wilde, Freud to Foucault.* Oxford: Clarendon Press, 1991.

Durston, Christopher. "Puritan Rule and the Failure of Cultural Revolution, 1645-1660." In *The Culture of English Puritanism, 1560-1700*, ed. Christopher Durston and Jacqueline Eales, 210-33, notes 312-16. New York: St Martin's Press, 1996.

Ebner, Dean. *Autobiography in Seventeenth-Century England: Theology and the Self.* The Hague: Mouton, 1971.

Eco, Umberto. *The Search for the Perfect Language*, trans. J. Feutress. Oxford, Blackwell, 1995.

Edwards, Karen L. "*Susannas Apologie* and the Politics of Privity." *Literature and History*, 3rd ser. 6. 1 (1997): 1-6.

Elsky, Martin. *Authorizing Words: Speech, Writing, and Print in the English Renaissance.* Ithaca: Cornell University Press, 1989.

Farnell, James E. "The Usurpation of Honest London Householders: Barebone's Parliament." *English Historical Review* 82 (1967): 24-46.

Ferguson, Margaret W. "Renaissance Concepts of the 'Woman Writer'." In *Women and Literature in Britain 1500-1700*, ed. Helen Wilcox, 143-68. Cambridge: Cambridge University Press, 1996.

Firth, Katharine R. *The Apocalyptic Tradition in Reformation Britain, 1580-1645.* Oxford: Oxford University Press, 1979.

Foster, Joseph. *Alumni Oxonienses: The Members of the University of Oxford 1500-1714.* 4 vols. Oxford: James Palmer and Co., 1891.

Fraser, Antonia. *Cromwell: Our Chief of Men.* London: Weidenfeld and Nicolson, 1973.

———. *The Weaker Vessel: Woman's Lot in Seventeenth-Century England.* London: Weidenfeld and Nicolson, 1984.

Freedman, David Noel, ed. *The Anchor Bible Dictionary.* New York and London: Doubleday, 1992.

Friedman, Jerome. *Miracles and the Pulp Press During the English Revolution.* London: UCL Press, 1993. (U.S. title: *The Battle of the Frogs and Fairford's Flies.*)

Fuller, Thomas. *The History of the Worthies of England*, new ed. by P. Austin Nuttall. 3 vols. New York: AMS Press Inc., 1965.

Gaunt, Peter. *Oliver Cromwell.* Oxford: Blackwell, 1996.

Gentles, Ian. *The New Model Army in England, Ireland and Scotland, 1645-1653.* Oxford: Blackwell, 1992.

Gibbs, V. *The Complete Peerage of England, Scotland, Ireland, Great Britain and the United Kingdom.* 13 vols. London: The St Catherine's Press, 1916.

Gibson, K. "Apocalyptic and Millenarian Prophecy in Early Stuart Europe: Philip Ziegler, Ludwig Friedrich Giffthiel and the Fifth Monarchy." In *Prophecy: The Power of Inspired Language in History 1300-2000*, ed. Bertrand Taithe and Tim Thornton, 71-83. Stroud, Glos.: Sutton Publishing, 1997.

Goldingay, John E. *Word Biblical Commentary*, vol. 30: *Daniel*. Dallas, TX: Word Books, 1989.

Graff, Harvey J., ed. *Literacy and Social Development in the West: A Reader*. Cambridge: Cambridge University Press, 1981.

Graham, Elspeth, Hilary Hinds, Elaine Hobby, and Helen Wilcox, eds. *Her Own Life: Autobiographical Writings by Seventeenth-Century English-women*. London: Routledge, 1989.

Graham, Elspeth. "Authority, Resistance and Loss: Gendered Difference in the Writings of John Bunyan and Hannah Allen." In *John Bunyan and his England, 1628–88*, ed. Anne Laurence, W. R. Owens, and Stuart Sim, 115–30. London and Ronceverte: The Hambledon Press, 1990.

———. "Women's Writing and the Self." In *Women and Literature in Britain 1500–1700*, ed. Helen Wilcox, 209–33. Cambridge: Cambridge University Press, 1996.

Grant, Robert M. *A Short History of the Interpretation of the Bible*, 2nd ed. London: Adam & Charles Black, 1965.

Gray, John. *The New Century Bible Commentary: Joshua, Judges, Ruth*. Basingstoke: Marshall, Morgan and Scott Publications Ltd., 1986.

Greaves, Richard L. and Robert Zaller, eds. *Biographical Dictionary of British Radicals in the Seventeenth Century*. 3 vols. Brighton: Harvester, 1982–84.

Greenblatt, Stephen. *Renaissance Self-Fashioning: From More to Shakespeare*. Chicago and London: University of Chicago Press, 1980.

Hainsworth, Roger. *The Swordsmen in Power: War and Politics under the English Republic 1649–1660*. Stroud, Glos.: Sutton Publishing, 1997.

Hibbert, Christopher. *Cavaliers and Roundheads: The English at War 1642–1649*. London: BCA/HarperCollins, 1993.

Hill, Christopher. *God's Englishman: Oliver Cromwell and the English Revolution*. London: Weidenfeld and Nicolson, 1970.

———. *The World Turned Upside Down: Radical Ideas During the English Revolution*. 2nd ed. Harmondsworth: Penguin, 1975.

———. *The Century of Revolution 1603–1714*. 2nd ed. Walton-on-Thames: Nelson, 1980.

———. *Antichrist in Seventeenth-Century England*. 2nd ed. London: Verso, 1990.

———. *The English Bible and the Seventeenth-Century English Revolution*. London: Allen Lane/The Penguin Press, 1993.

Hinds, Hilary. *God's Englishwomen: Seventeenth-Century Radical Sectarian Writing and Feminist Criticism*. Manchester: Manchester University Press, 1996.

Hobbes, Thomas. *Behemoth, or The Long Parliament (1682)*, ed. Ferdinand Tönnies; introd. Stephen Holmes. Chicago and London: University of Chicago Press, 1990.

Hobby, Elaine. _Virtue of Necessity: English Women's Writing 1649-1688._ London: Virago, 1988.

——. "The Politics of Women's Prophecy in the English Revolution." In _Sacred and Profane: Secular and Devotional Interplay in Early Modern British Literature,_ ed. Helen Wilcox et al., 295-306. Amsterdam: Free University Press, 1996.

Houlbrooke, Ralph. "The Puritan Death-bed, c. 1560-c. 1660." In _The Culture of English Puritanism, 1560-1700,_ ed. Christopher Durston and Jacqueline Eales, 122-44, notes 299-301. New York: St Martin's Press, 1996.

Hunter, J. Paul. _Before Novels: The Cultural Contexts of Eighteenth-Century English Fiction._ New York: W. W. Norton, 1990.

Hutchinson, Lucy. _Memoirs of the Life of Colonel Hutchinson._ London: Kegan, Paul, Trench, Trubner and Co., 1904.

Jeffs, Robin, ed. _The English Revolution III. Newsbooks 5, volume 13. Mercurius Politicus 1656,_ reproductions in facsimile with notes by Peter Thomas. London: Cornmarket Press, 1971.

Johnson, David J. _Southwark and the City._ London: Oxford University Press, 1969.

Jordan, Constance. _Renaissance Feminism: Literary Texts and Political Models._ Ithaca and London: Cornell University Press, 1990.

Kendall, R. T. _Calvin and English Calvinism to 1649._ Oxford: Oxford University Press, 1977.

Kishlansky, Mark A. _The Rise of the New Model Army._ Cambridge: Cambridge University Press, 1979.

Lamont, William. _Puritanism and Historical Controversy._ London: UCL Press, 1996.

Langbauer, Laurie. _Women and Romance: The Consolations of Gender in the English Novel._ Ithaca: Cornell University Press, 1990.

Laurence, Anne. _Women in England 1500-1760: A Social History._ London: Weidenfeld and Nicolson, 1994.

Laymon, Charles M., ed. _The Interpreter's One-Volume Commentary on the Bible._ London and Glasgow: Collins, 1972.

Le Neve, John. _Fasti Ecclesiae Anglicanae 1541-1857._ vol. 1, comp. Joyce M. Horn. London: Athlone Press, 1969.

Lilley, Kate. "Blazing Worlds: Seventeenth-Century Women's Utopian Writing." In _Women, Texts and Histories 1575-1760,_ ed. Clare Brant and Diane Purkiss, 102-33. London: Routledge, 1992.

Lindley, Keith. _Popular Politics and Religion in Civil War London._ Aldershot: Scolar Press, 1997.

MacDonald, Michael. _Mystical Bedlam: Madness, Anxiety, and Healing in Seventeenth-Century England._ Cambridge: Cambridge University Press, 1981.

Mack, Phyllis. "Women as Prophets during the English Civil War." In *The Origins of Anglo-American Radicalism*, ed. Margaret Jacob and James Jacob, 214–30. London: George Allen and Unwin, 1984.

——. "The Prophet and Her Audience: Gender and Knowledge in The World Turned Upside Down." In *Reviving the English Revolution: Reflections and Elaborations on the Work of Christopher Hill*, ed. Geoff Eley and William Hunt, 139–52. London: Verso, 1988.

——. *Visionary Women: Ecstatic Prophecy in Seventeenth-Century England*. Berkeley: University of California Press, 1992.

Maclean, Ian. *The Renaissance Notion of Woman: A Study in the Fortunes of Scholasticism and Medical Science in European Intellectual Life*. Cambridge: Cambridge University Press, 1980.

Mason, Mary G. "The Other Voice: Autobiographies of Women Writers." In *Life/Lines: Theorizing Women's Autobiography*, ed. Bella Brodzki and Celeste Schenck, 19–44. Ithaca and London: Cornell University Press, 1988.

Matthews, A. G. *Calamy Revised: Being a Version of Edmund Calamy's Account of the Ministers and Others Ejected and Silenced, 1660–2*. Oxford: Clarendon Press, 1934.

Mayes, A. D. H. *Judges*. Sheffield: JSOT Press, 1985.

Metzger, Bruce M. *An Introduction to the Apocrypha*. New York: Oxford University Press, 1957.

Modleski, Tania. *Loving With a Vengeance: Mass-Produced Fantasies for Women*. London: Methuen, 1982.

Morrill, John, ed. *The Impact of the English Civil War*. London: Collins and Brown, 1991.

——, ed. *Revolution and Restoration: England in the 1650s*. London: Collins and Brown, 1992.

——. *The Nature of the English Revolution*. Harlow: Longman, 1993.

Morton, A. L. *The World of the Ranters: Religious Radicalism in the English Revolution*. London: Lawrence and Wishart, 1970.

Neal, Daniel. *The History of the Puritans; or Protestant Nonconformists*. 5 vols. London: William Baynes and Son, 1822.

Nuttall, Geoffrey. *The Welsh Saints, 1640–1660: Walter Cradock, Vavasor Powell, Morgan Llwyd*. Cardiff: University of Wales Press, 1957.

——. *Visible Saints: The Congregational Way 1640–1660*. Oxford: Basil Blackwell, 1957.

Osborn, James M. *The Beginnings of Autobiography in England*. Berkeley: University of California Press, 1959.

Paster, Gail Kern. *The Body Embarrassed: Drama and the Disciplines of Shame in Early Modern England*. Ithaca: Cornell University Press, 1993.

Paul, Robert S. *The Lord Protector: Religion and Politics in the Life of Oliver Cromwell*. Grand Rapids, MI: William B. Eerdmans Publishing Co., 1955.

Pearl, Valerie. *London and the Outbreak of the Puritan Revolution: City Government and National Politics, 1625–43*. Oxford: Oxford University Press, 1961.

Pease, Donald E. "Author." In *Critical Terms for Literary Study*, 2nd ed., ed. Frank Lentricchia and Thomas McLaughlin, 105–17. Chicago and London: University of Chicago Press, 1995.

Pooley, Roger. "Grace Abounding and the New Sense of the Self." In *John Bunyan and His England, 1628–88*, ed. Anne Laurence, W. R. Owens, and Stuart Sim, 105–14. London and Ronceverte: The Hambledon Press, 1990.

Prockter, Adrian, and Robert Taylor. *The A to Z of Elizabethan London*. London: London Topographical Society, 1979.

Purkiss, Diane. "Producing the Voice, Consuming the Body: Women Prophets of the Seventeenth Century." In *Women, Writing, History 1640–1740*, ed. Isobel Grundy and Susan Wiseman, 139–58. London: Batsford, 1992.

Radford, Jean, ed. *The Progress of Romance: The Politics of Popular Fiction*. London: Routledge and Kegan Paul, 1986.

Radway, Janice. *Reading the Romance: Women, Patriarchy and Popular Literature*. Chapel Hill and London: University of North Carolina Press, 1984.

Reay, Barry. "Radicalism and Religion in the English Revolution: An Introduction." In *Radical Religion in the English Revolution*, ed. J. F. McGregor and B. Reay, 1–21. Oxford: Oxford University Press, 1984.

Rogers, Edward. *Some Account of the Life and Opinions of a Fifth-Monarchy Man. Chiefly Extracted from the Writings of John Rogers, Preacher*. London: Longman, Green, Reader and Dyer, 1867.

Rogers, P. G. *The Fifth Monarchy Men*. London: Oxford University Press, 1966.

Room, Adrian. *The Street Names of England*. Stanford, Eng.: Paul Watkins, 1992.

Russell, D. S. *The Method and Message of Jewish Apocalyptic*. London: SCM Press, 1964.

Sawday, Jonathan. *The Body Emblazoned: Dissection and the Human Body in Renaissance Culture*. London and New York: Routledge, 1995.

Schwoerer, Lois G. *"No Standing Armies!": The Antiarmy Ideology in Seventeenth-Century England*. Baltimore and London: The Johns Hopkins University Press, 1974.

Sharpe, Kevin. "An Image Doting Rabble: The Failure of Republican Culture in Seventeenth-Century England." In *Refiguring Revolutions: Aesthetics and Politics from the English Revolution to the Romantic Revolution*, ed. Kevin Sharpe and Steven N. Zwicker, 25–56, notes 302–11. Berkeley, Los Angeles, London: University of California Press, 1998.

——— and Steven N. Zwicker. "Politics of Discourse: Introduction." In *Politics of Discourse: The Literature and History of Seventeenth-Century England*, ed. Kevin Sharpe and Steven N. Zwicker, 1-20, notes 297-300. Berkeley, Los Angeles, and London: University of California Press, 1987.

Sharpe, Reginald R. *London and the Kingdom: A History*. 3 vols. London: Longman, Green and Co., 1894.

Sherwood, Roy. *The Court of Oliver Cromwell*. London: Croom Helm, 1977.

———. *Oliver Cromwell: King In All But Name 1653-1658*. Stroud, Glos.: Sutton Publishing, 1997.

Smith, Nigel, ed. *A Collection of Ranter Writings from the Seventeenth Century*. London: Junction Books, 1983.

———. *Perfection Proclaimed: Language and Literature in English Radical Religion 1640-1660*. Oxford: Clarendon Press, 1989.

Smith, Sidonie. *A Poetics of Women's Autobiography: Marginality and the Fictions of Self-Representation*. Bloomington: Indiana University Press, 1987.

Sommerville, C. John. *Popular Religion in Restoration England*. Gainesville: University of Florida Press, 1977.

Sommerville, Margaret R. *Sex and Subjection: Attitudes to Women in Early-Modern Society*. London: Arnold, 1995.

Stallybrass, Peter. "Patriarchal Territories: The Body Enclosed." In *Rewriting the Renaissance: The Discourses of Sexual Difference in Early-Modern Europe*, ed. Margaret W. Ferguson, Maureen Quilligan, and Nancy J. Vickers, 123-42, notes 344-47. Chicago and London: University of Chicago Press, 1986.

Sugden, Edward H. *A Topographical Dictionary to the Works of Shakespeare and his Fellow Dramatists*. Manchester: Manchester University Press, 1925.

Taithe, B., and T. Thornton. "The Language of History: Past and Future in Prophecy." In *Prophecy: The Power of Inspired Language in History 1300-2000*, ed. Bertrand Taithe and Tim Thornton, 1-14. Stroud, Glos.: Sutton Publishing, 1997.

Thomas, Keith. "Women and the Civil War Sects." *Past and Present* 13 (1958): 42-62.

———. *Religion and the Decline of Magic*. London: Weidenfeld and Nicolson, 1971.

Thompson, Edward. "On the Rant." In *Reviving the English Revolution: Reflections and Elaborations on the Work of Christopher Hill*, ed. Geoff Eley and William Hunt, 153-60. London: Verso, 1988.

Thomson, John A. F. *The Later Lollards 1414-1520*. Oxford: Oxford University Press, 1965.

Thornton, T. "Reshaping the Local Future: The Development and Uses of Provincial Political Prophecies, 1300–1900." In *Prophecy: The Power of Inspired Language in History 1300–2000*, ed. Bertrand Taithe and Tim Thornton, 51–67. Stroud, Glos.: Sutton Publishing, 1997.

Tillyard, E. M. W. *The Elizabethan World Picture.* London: Chatto and Windus, 1943.

Tindall, William York. *John Bunyan, Mechanick Preacher.* Columbia University Studies in English and Comparative Literature. New York: Columbia University Press, 1934.

Todd, Margo, ed. *Reformation to Revolution: Politics and Religion in Early Modern England.* London: Routledge, 1995.

Toon, Peter, ed. *Puritans, The Millennium and the Future of Israel: Puritan Eschatology 1600–1660.* Cambridge and London: James Clarke and Co. Ltd., 1970.

Traub, Valerie. "Gendering Mortality in Early Modern Anatomies." In *Feminist Readings of Early Modern Culture: Emerging Subjects*, ed. Valerie Traub, M. Lindsay Kaplan, and Dympna Callaghan, 44–92. Cambridge: Cambridge University Press, 1996.

Trill, Suzanne. "Religion and the Construction of Femininity." In *Women and Literature in Britain 1500–1700*, ed. Helen Wilcox, 30–55. Cambridge: Cambridge University Press, 1996.

Turner, James Grantham, ed. *Sexuality and Gender in Early Modern Europe: Institutions, Texts, Images.* Cambridge: Cambridge University Press, 1993.

Underdown, David. *Pride's Purge: Politics in the Puritan Revolution.* Oxford: Clarendon Press, 1971.

Venn, J., and J. A. Venn. *Alumni Cantabrigienses.* 4 vols. Cambridge: Cambridge University Press, 1922–27.

von Rohr, John. *The Covenant of Grace in Puritan Thought.* Atlanta: Scholars Press, 1986.

Watkins, Owen. *The Puritan Experience: Studies in Spiritual Autobiography.* London: Routledge & Kegan Paul, 1972.

Watt, Diane. *Secretaries of God: Women Prophets in Late Medieval and Early Modern England.* Cambridge: D. S. Brewer, 1997.

Webster, Charles. *The Great Instauration: Science, Medicine and Reform 1626–1660.* London: Duckworth, 1975.

Weinreb, Ben, and Christopher Hibbert, eds. *The London Encyclopaedia.* London: Macmillan, 1983.

Wheale, Nigel. *Writing and Society: Literacy, Print and Politics in Britain 1590–1660.* London and New York: Routledge, 1999.

Wheatley, Henry B. *London, Past and Present: Its History, Associations and Traditions.* 3 vols. London: John Murray, 1891.

Whitebrook, J. C., ed. *London Citizens in 1651. Being a Transcript of Harleian Ms. 4778.* London: A. W. Cannon and Co., 1910.

Wilcox, Helen. "Private Writing and Public Function: Autobiographical Texts by Renaissance Englishwomen." In *Gloriana's Face: Women, Public and Private, in the English Renaissance*, ed. S. P. Cerasano and Marion Wynne-Davies, 47–62. Hemel Hempstead: Harvester Wheatsheaf, 1992.

Williams, Raymond. *Keywords: A Vocabulary of Culture and Society.* London: Fontana, 1976.

Wilson, Walter. *The History and Antiquities of Dissenting Churches and Meeting Houses in London, Westminster, and Southwark, including the Lives of their Ministers, from the Rise of Nonconformity to the Present Time.* 4 vols. London, 1814.

Wing, Donald. *Short-Title Catalogue of Books Printed in England, Scotland, Ireland, Wales, and British America, and of English Books Printed in Other Countries, 1641–1700*, rev. and ed. John J. Morrison et al. New York: Modern Language Association of America, 1972–88.

Wiseman, Sue. "Unsilent Instruments and the Devil's Cushions: Authority in Seventeenth-Century Women's Prophetic Discourse." In *New Feminist Discourses: Critical Essays on Theories and Texts*, ed. Isobel Armstrong, 176–96. London: Routledge, 1992.

Wolff, Janet. "The Invisible Flâneuse: Women and the Literature of Modernity." In Wolff, *Feminine Sentences: Essays on Women and Culture*, 34–50. Cambridge: Polity Press, 1990.

Wood, Anthony. *Athenae Oxonienses*, ed. Philip Bliss. 4 vols.; facsimile of 1813–1820 ed. Hildesheim: Olms, 1969.

Woodhouse, A. S. P., ed. *Puritanism and Liberty: Being the Army Debates (1647–9) from the Clarke Manuscripts with Supplementary Documents.* London: Dent, 1938, repr. 1974.

Woolrych, Austin. "The Calling of Barebone's Parliament." *English Historical Review* 80 (1965): 492–513.

———. *Commonwealth to Protectorate.* Oxford: Clarendon Press, 1982.

Worden, Blair. "The Bill for a New Representative." *English Historical Review* 86 (1971): 473–96.

———. *The Rump Parliament 1648–1653.* London: Cambridge University Press, 1974.

———. "Providence and Politics in Cromwellian England." *Past and Present* 109 (1985): 55–99.

INDEX TO THE INTRODUCTION